Quick & Easy
family favorites

Creamy Banana Pudding,
page 302

Quick & Easy
family favorites

Oxmoor House

Quick & Easy
family favorites

©2009 by Gooseberry Patch
600 London Road, Delaware, Ohio 43015
1-800-854-6673, **www.gooseberrypatch.com**
©2009 by Oxmoor House, Inc.
Book Division of Southern Progress Corporation
P.O. Box 2262, Birmingham, Alabama 35201-2262

Hardcover ISBN-13: 978-0-8487-3299-8
Hardcover ISBN-10: 0-8487-3299-5
Softcover ISBN-13: 978-0-8487-3308-7
Softcover ISBN-10: 0-8487-3308-8
Library of Congress Control Number: 2009925696
Printed in the United States of America
First Printing 2009

Oxmoor House, Inc.
VP, Publishing Director: Jim Childs
Editorial Director: Susan Payne Dobbs
Brand Manager: Terri Laschober Robertson
Managing Editor: L. Amanda Owens

Gooseberry Patch Quick & Easy Family Favorites
Editor: Kelly Hooper Troiano
Project Editor: Emily Chappell
Senior Designer: Melissa Jones Clark
Director, Test Kitchens: Elizabeth Tyler Austin
Assistant Director, Test Kitchens: Julie Christopher
Test Kitchens Professionals: Kathleen Royal Phillips,
    Catherine Crowell Steele, Ashley T. Strickland
Photography Director: Jim Bathie
Senior Photo Stylist: Kay E. Clarke
Associate Photo Stylist: Katherine Eckert Coyne
Senior Production Manager: Greg A. Amason

Contributors
Copy Editor: Jasmine Hodges
Proofreader: Lauren Brooks
Interns: Wendy Ball, Christine Taylor
Food Stylists: Ana Price Kelly, Debby Maugans
Photographers: Beau Gustafson, Lee Harrelson,
    Becky Luiguart-Staynor
Photo Stylists: Missy Neville Crawford, Jan Guatro

Time Inc. Home Entertainment
Publisher: Richard Fraiman
General Manager: Steven Sandonato
Executive Director, Marketing Services: Carol Pittard
Executive Director, Retail and Special Sales: Tom Mifsud
Director, New Product Development: Peter Harper
Director, Publicity: Sydney Webber
Assistant Director, Newsstand Marketing: Laura Adam
Assistant Publishing Director, Brand Marketing: Joy Butts
Associate Counsel: Helen Wan

To order additional publications, call 1-800-765-6400.
For more books to enrich your life, visit **oxmoorhouse.com**
To search, savor and share thousands of recipes, visit **myrecipes.com**

Cover: Easy Chicken Pot Pie (page 126)

Dear Friend,

Is it possible to have family favorite recipes that are also quick & easy? You bet! Even on the busiest of days, you and your family can enjoy a delicious, homecooked meal...with a scrumptious, quick & easy dessert! Take a peek at the Chocolate-Chip Pudding Cake on page 282...only 3 ingredients and it cooks in 35 minutes!

With simple ingredient lists, quick cook times and items you already have in your pantry, gathering your family 'round the table is a snap with winners like Easy Chicken Pot Pie (page 126) and Country-Fried Steak (page 145). And cooking gets even easier with a special chapter that's devoted to recipes with 5 ingredients or less. Don't miss the 2-ingredient Orange Sherbet Ice Cream (page 81). For those busy weeknights, try breakfast for dinner. These no-fuss foods make it the perfect way to end your day. Savory Stuffed French Toast (page 106) or Scrumptious Blueberry Pancakes (page 109) will be a hands-down favorite every time.

For simple snacks, warming soups, delicious sandwiches and speedy sides, it doesn't get any easier, or quicker, than our fast-fix recipes. We even think slow cooking is fast! Talk about ease...just toss together your ingredients in the crock in the morning, and by evening, supper is ready. Be sure to satisfy your family's sweet tooth the oh-so-simple way with our yummy collection of treats beginning on page 273. You'll find the perfect ending to any meal.

So take a look inside...you'll find lots of how-to's and clever ideas for keeping meals easy and delicious. You'll read what our friends have to say about their tried & true recipes as they share their own quick tips and memories. It's all about being together, and now, mealtime just got easier!

From our families to yours,

Vickie & JoAnn

Contents

Sticky Buns, page 113

Lillian's Beef Stew, page 209

Southern Pork Barbecue, page 153

No-Fry Fried Ice Cream, page 305

Munchable Snack Mix,
page 19

snacks
in a snap

For simple snacks or party food in a hurry, this chapter has what you're looking for. Lunchbox treats like Kiddies' Favorite Trail Mix (page 43) will keep the young ones charged throughout the day. Let the kids prepare chocolatey Marshmallow Pops (page 41)...don't forget the festive toppings! For gathering with family & friends, check out our twist on the cheese ball...mini Party Cheese Balls (page 17). Fancy or simple...these snacks are all quick & easy!

Vickie's Gazpacho Dip

Fresh summer flavors burst from each scoop of this chunky dip. Tortilla chips are a good choice for dipping.

3 tomatoes, diced
3 avocados, peeled, pitted and
    diced
4 green onions, thinly sliced
4.5-oz. can diced green chiles,
    undrained

3 T. olive oil
1½ T. cider vinegar
1 t. garlic salt
½ t. salt
¼ t. pepper

Combine tomatoes, avocados, onions and chiles in a large bowl; set aside. Whisk together olive oil and remaining 4 ingredients; drizzle over vegetables and toss well. Cover and chill. Makes 5 cups.

Vickie
Gooseberry Patch

make it festive!

No one can resist fresh salsa and chips. Pile blue and yellow tortilla chips in a colorful bowl placed in the middle of a large plate or platter. Don't forget the tangy homemade salsa!

Cream Cheese Apple Dip

Offer marshmallows and pretzels alongside apple slices to go with this creamy dip.

8-oz. pkg. cream cheese,
    softened
¼ c. sugar
¾ c. brown sugar, packed

1 t. vanilla extract
½ c. toffee baking bits
apple slices

"You won't be able to stop dipping into this creamy concoction!"

Staci

Blend together cream cheese and sugars; mix in vanilla. Stir in toffee bits. Serve at room temperature with apple slices. Store in refrigerator. Makes about 2 cups.

Staci Meyers
Cocoa, FL

no more browning

You probably know that lemon juice keeps apple slices from browning, but did you know that lemon-lime soda works just as well?

Fruit Salsa with Cinnamon Chips

Kiwis, apples, raspberries and strawberries make up this colorful salsa. It'll be a treat that guests will not want to miss…especially when served with homemade cinnamon-flavored chips.

2 kiwi, peeled and diced
2 Golden Delicious apples,
 cored, peeled and diced
½ lb. raspberries
16-oz. pkg. strawberries, hulled
 and diced
1 c. plus 2 T. sugar, divided

1 T. brown sugar, packed
3 T. strawberry preserves
1 to 2 T. cinnamon
10 (10-inch) flour tortillas,
 sliced into wedges
butter-flavored non-stick
 vegetable spray

Combine all fruit in a large bowl; mix in 2 tablespoons sugar, brown sugar and strawberry preserves. Cover and chill at least 15 minutes.

Mix together remaining one cup sugar and cinnamon. Arrange tortilla wedges in a single layer on an ungreased baking sheet; coat chips with butter-flavored vegetable spray. Sprinkle with desired amount of cinnamon-sugar.

Bake at 350 degrees for 8 to 10 minutes. Repeat with remaining tortilla wedges; cool 15 minutes. Serve chips with chilled fruit mixture. Makes 10 to 15 servings.

Ashley Connelly
Louisa, VA

"I made this for our Sunday morning church refreshments and it was a huge hit. I also like to take this to bridal and baby showers."

Ashley

Macadamia Nut Dip

Prepared horseradish lends a pungent bite to this otherwise mild and creamy appetizer.

8-oz. pkg. cream cheese, softened
½ c. sour cream
1 c. macadamia nuts, chopped

2 T. prepared horseradish
2 green onions, minced
⅛ t. garlic salt
assorted crackers

Mix together all ingredients except crackers; chill. Serve with crackers. Makes 6 to 10 servings.

Judy Borecky
Escondido, CA

Hot Chili Cheese Dip

Be sure to have this hearty, cheesy dip on your menu the next time family & friends are over to watch the big game...it'll be a hit.

1 lb. mild or spicy ground pork sausage, browned and drained
2 (10¾-oz.) cans nacho cheese soup
15-oz. can chili without beans

14½-oz. can tomatoes with chiles
16-oz. pkg. pasteurized process cheese spread, cubed

Combine all ingredients except cheese in a large saucepan over medium heat; cook until bubbly. Add cheese. Reduce heat; cook and stir until cheese is completely melted. Makes 6 to 7 cups.

David Wink
Gooseberry Patch

Super Nachos

Keep these simple ingredients around for a quick & easy snack the whole family will enjoy.

2 (10-inch) flour tortillas
¾ c. salsa
4.5-oz. can green chiles, drained
    and diced

½ c. sliced black olives
1 c. shredded Monterey Jack
    cheese

"So quick...makes a great snack or even lunch."

Mary

Place tortillas on an ungreased baking sheet; spread salsa over tortillas. Sprinkle chiles and olives over salsa; top with cheese.

Bake at 425 degrees for 10 minutes or until tortillas are crisp and cheese is melted. Use a pizza cutter to slice each into 8 wedges. Makes 8 appetizer servings.

Mary Murray
Gooseberry Patch

veggie kabobs

Guests will love these dippers. Thread carrot and celery slices, cauliflower and broccoli flowerets, and olives onto small wooden skewers in different combinations…arrange around yummy dips and enjoy!

Party Cheese Balls

For a festive presentation, roll up this flavorful mixture into 7 mini cheese balls as pictured opposite. For just one, proceed as directed in the recipe, rolling mixture into one large ball.

2 (8-oz.) pkgs. cream cheese,
    softened
2 c. shredded sharp Cheddar
    cheese
1 t. pimento, chopped
1 t. onion, minced

1 t. lemon juice
1 t. green pepper, chopped
2 t. Worcestershire sauce
⅛ t. cayenne pepper
⅛ t. salt
Optional: chopped pecans

"Everyone will be going back for more, so be sure to have plenty of crackers... these cheese balls are simply addictive!"

Sarah

Blend cream cheese until light and fluffy; add Cheddar cheese and next 7 ingredients. Shape into 7 mini balls (about one cup each); wrap in plastic wrap and refrigerate until firm. Roll in pecans, if desired. Makes 7 mini balls.

Sarah Sommers
Atwater, CA

mini servings

Serve mini cheese balls in paper muffin cups. Fill more paper muffin cups with crackers and pretzels and arrange alongside mini cheese balls...guests can enjoy one of each.

Pizza Crescent Snacks

Offer a pizza buffet line. Put all the ingredients in separate bowls, and let everyone create their own pizza.

8-oz. tube refrigerated crescent
   rolls
14-oz. jar pizza sauce

¾ c. sliced pepperoni
¾ c. sliced mushrooms
1 c. shredded mozzarella cheese

Unroll crescent rolls into individual triangles on an ungreased baking sheet. Spread a layer of pizza sauce over dough and top with pepperoni and mushrooms. Sprinkle cheese on top; roll up into crescent shape.

Bake at 375 degrees for 18 to 25 minutes or until rolls are golden and cheese is bubbling. Makes 8 appetizers.

Beth Flack
Terre Haute, IN

tailgating fun

Everybody loves a tailgating party…and a small-town college rivalry can be just as much fun as a Big Ten game. Load up a pickup truck with tasty finger foods, sandwich fixin's and a big washtub full of bottled drinks on ice. It's all about food and fun!

Munchable Snack Mix

(pictured on page 8)

This sweet-and-salty mix is ideal to take along for a road trip. It's a snack that will appeal to savory and sweet lovers alike.

2 (12-oz.) pkgs. candy-coated
   chocolate mini-baking bits
12-oz. can salted peanuts

11-oz. pkg. butterscotch chips
2 c. raisins
1 c. cashews

Combine all ingredients in a large mixing bowl; mix well. Place in plastic zipping bags. Makes 9 cups.

Coralita Truax
Loudonville, OH

Ranch Pretzel Bites

This snack mix is a variation on one that uses oyster crackers. Whichever you use, eat up, because it won't last for long!

16-oz. pkg. large pretzels
2-oz. pkg. ranch salad
   dressing mix

¾ c. oil
1½ t. garlic powder
1½ t. dill weed

"Enjoy during your favorite movie!"

Susan

Break pretzels into bite-size pieces; place in a large mixing bowl. Combine remaining ingredients in a separate mixing bowl and pour over pretzels; toss to coat. Pour onto an ungreased baking sheet.

Bake at 200 degrees for one hour, stirring every 15 minutes. Makes 16 servings.

Note: Small bite-size pretzels may be substituted for the large pretzels.

Susan Young
Madison, AL

Cheese Bread Bites

Make up a double batch of these yummy bites to have on hand for unexpected company…or for yourself for snacking! They're a handy snack because you can bake just a few at a time when you want them.

12-oz. loaf French bread, crusts
  trimmed
1 c. butter
½ lb. sharp Cheddar cheese,
  cubed

2 (3-oz.) pkgs. cream cheese,
  softened
4 egg whites, stiffly beaten
Optional: marinara sauce

Cut bread into one-inch cubes; set aside. Melt butter and cheeses in a double boiler over low heat, stirring often. Remove from heat; fold in egg whites. Dip bread cubes into cheese mixture; set on greased baking sheets. Place in freezer until frozen; remove from baking sheets and store in plastic zipping bags in the freezer up to one month.

To serve, bake frozen bites at 400 degrees for 12 minutes on greased baking sheets. Serve with marinara sauce, if desired. Serves 8 to 10.

Nola Laflin
Coral Springs, FL

"I like simple and easy make-ahead recipes. This is a favorite of my grandchildren and family. When they tell me when they're flying into Florida, I start making and storing these right away!"

Nola

Crispy Parmesan Pita Crackers

These are great with salads and dips. For added flavor, sprinkle with garlic powder or dried herbs before baking.

5 pita rounds   ½ c. grated Parmesan cheese
no-stick vegetable spray

   Split pitas and cut each half into 6 wedges. Arrange on a baking sheet; spray lightly with non-stick vegetable spray and sprinkle with grated Parmesan. Bake at 450 degrees for 8 to 10 minutes or until crisp. Makes 5 dozen.

Laura Fuller
Fort Wayne, IN

dippers

Try serving "light" dippers with hearty full-flavored dips and spreads. Fresh veggies, pita wedges, baked tortilla chips and multi-grain crispbread are all sturdy enough to scoop up dips yet won't overshadow the flavor of the dip.

Blue Cheese Cut-Out Crackers

These delicate cheese wafers carry a touch of hot pepper...but you can season to your own taste.

1 c. all-purpose flour
7 T. crumbled blue cheese
1 egg yolk
4 t. whipping cream

7 T. butter, softened
½ t. dried parsley
⅛ tsp. salt
cayenne pepper to taste

Mix all ingredients in a bowl; let rest for 30 minutes. Roll dough out to ⅛-inch thickness. Use your favorite cookie cutter shapes to cut out the crackers. Bake on ungreased baking sheets at 400 degrees for 8 to 10 minutes or just until golden. Carefully remove the delicate crackers when cool. Makes 1½ to 2 dozen.

party crudités

Set out pretty bowls of these crackers alongside nuts, olives, fruit, salsas and chips, veggies and dip for snacks everyone will love.

Tomato-Bacon Nibbles

A ¼-teaspoon measuring spoon is just right for scooping out tiny tomatoes for stuffing.

24 to 30 cherry tomatoes
16-oz. pkg. bacon, crisply cooked
   and crumbled
2 T. fresh parsley, chopped

½ c. green onions, finely chopped
3 T. grated Parmesan cheese
½ c. mayonnaise

Cut a thin slice off the top of each tomato and, if desired, cut a thin slice from bottom of each tomato (so tomatoes will stand upright); scoop out and discard tomato pulp. Place tomatoes upside-down on a paper towel to drain 10 minutes.

Mix bacon and remaining 4 ingredients in a small bowl; stuff tomatoes. Serve immediately or chill up to 2 hours. Makes 2 to 2½ dozen.

Anna McMaster
Portland, OR

clever coolers

If you're entertaining outdoors, keep food chilled by placing ice cubes underneath or around your serving plate, as shown in this illustration.

Party Tortilla Wraps

Talk about versatile! These wraps are a great go-to for a tasty appetizer, a special treat for the lunchbox or a handy afternoon snack.

8-oz. container chive cream cheese
4 (10-inch) flour tortillas

1 lb. sliced cooked ham
8-oz. pkg. shredded American cheese

Spread cream cheese evenly over tortillas. Place several slices of ham on each tortilla; sprinkle with shredded cheese.

Roll up tortillas. Place in refrigerator for 15 minutes. Cut into one-inch pieces. Makes 40 appetizers.

Mandy Hardy
Middleville, MI

Chicken Bites

Once your kids get a taste of these crispy bites, they'll forgo the fast-food version!

4 boneless, skinless chicken breasts, cubed
½ c. mayonnaise

1 sleeve round buttery crackers, crushed

Toss chicken cubes in mayonnaise; roll in crushed crackers. Place on an aluminum foil-lined baking sheet and bake at 350 degrees for 10 minutes. Turn and bake another 10 minutes or until juices run clear when chicken is pierced with a fork. Makes 4 dozen appetizers.

Twila Koehn
Fruitland, ID

Hot Jalapeño Poppers

This is sure to be a favorite appetizer for those who love a bit of heat in every bite.

16 whole preserved jalapeño
    peppers
2 (8-oz.) pkgs. cream cheese,
    softened

1 egg, beaten
1 c. dry bread crumbs
¼ c. vegetable oil

Open the end of each pepper with a small knife to remove the stem and seeds. Using a pastry tube or small sandwich bag with one corner cut off, fill each pepper with cream cheese; coat peppers in beaten egg and then dip in bread crumbs.

Heat oil in a large skillet over medium heat; carefully place peppers in the pan and cook until golden, turning occasionally. Drain on paper towels. Serves 4.

savvy servers

Use tiered cake stands for bite-size appetizers...so handy, and they take up less space on the buffet table than setting out several serving platters.

Cheesy Potato Skins

Make a meal out of this by adding your favorite meat…barbecue pork, ham and chicken are all good choices.

4 potatoes, baked and halved
½ c. shredded Cheddar cheese
½ c. shredded mozzarella cheese

2 green onions, chopped
4 t. bacon bits

Place potatoes on an ungreased baking sheet; sprinkle with cheeses. Top with onions and bacon; heat under broiler until cheese melts. Serves 4 to 8.

Dolores Brock
Wellton, AZ

"We love to dip these potato skins in ranch dressing."

Dolores

Italian Eggplant Sticks

Served with marinara sauce or even salsa, this Italian-seasoned veggie will get a big thumbs-up from family & friends.

3 eggplant, peeled
1 c. Italian-flavored dry bread
  crumbs
1 t. salt

1 t. pepper
3 eggs
¼ c. milk
oil for deep frying

Cut eggplant into 3"x½" sticks; place in ice water for 30 minutes. Drain and set aside.

Combine bread crumbs, salt and pepper; set aside. Blend together eggs and milk in a shallow bowl; dip eggplant sticks into egg mixture and dredge in bread crumb mixture. Arrange eggplant on an ungreased baking sheet. Cover and chill 30 minutes.

Pour oil to a depth of one inch in a deep skillet; heat oil to 375 degrees. Add eggplant and cook 2 minutes on each side or until golden. Drain on paper towels. Serves 6.

Karen Pilcher
Burleson, TX

appetizer party

Family & friends will love an appetizer party! And if they have different tastes, don't worry about deciding on the perfect main dish...just serve 4 to 5 different appetizers and everyone can choose their favorites.

Grape Jelly Meatballs

Meatballs are always a crowd-pleaser...especially this version that uses grape jelly. Serve them in a slow cooker to keep them warm.

1 lb. ground beef
½ c. soft bread crumbs
1 egg
1 t. salt
½ t. pepper
½ t. seasoned salt
¼ t. garlic powder

½ c. instant rice, uncooked
2 onions, minced and divided
2 T. brown sugar, packed
14-oz. bottle catsup
¾ c. grape jelly
½ t. Worcestershire sauce

"Everyone should really try these... they're always a hit, with no leftovers."

Karrie

Combine first 8 ingredients in a bowl; add half the onions and mix well. Form mixture into one-inch balls. Arrange in an ungreased shallow baking pan; set aside.

Combine brown sugar and remaining 3 ingredients in a heavy saucepan; cook until jelly melts, stirring often. Pour jelly mixture over meatballs. Bake at 325 degrees for one hour. Serves 4 to 6.

Karrie Earley
Martinsburg, WV

Chinese Chicken Wings

Move over, hot wings. These Asian-inspired chicken wings are packed with flavor...and they're baked. Make extra, because the crowd will love them!

2 to 3 lbs. chicken wings
½ c. soy sauce
1 c. pineapple juice
⅓ c. brown sugar, packed
1 t. ground ginger
1 t. garlic salt
½ t. pepper
Optional: celery sticks and ranch
     salad dressing

Place wings in a large plastic zipping bag; set aside. Combine soy sauce and next 5 ingredients; pour over wings, turning to coat. Refrigerate overnight, turning several times.

Drain wings, discarding marinade; arrange in a single layer on an ungreased jelly-roll pan. Bake at 450 degrees for 25 to 30 minutes or until golden and juices run clear when chicken is pierced with a fork. Serve with celery and ranch dressing, if desired. Makes 2 to 2½ dozen.

Suzanne Erickson
Columbus, OH

Mini Sausage Tarts

These look so fancy on an appetizer tray. Your friends will never know how easy they are...that's your little secret!

1 lb. ground sausage, browned
    and drained
8-oz. pkg. shredded Mexican-
    blend cheese

1 c. ranch salad dressing
2 T. black olives, chopped
4 pkgs. frozen mini phyllo cups

Combine sausage, cheese, salad dressing and olives in a bowl; spoon a heaping teaspoonful of sausage mixture into each phyllo cup. Place cups on ungreased baking sheets; bake at 350 degrees for 10 to 12 minutes. Makes 5 dozen.

Wanda Boykin
Lewisburg, TN

early birds

Group a selection of appetizers on a small table separate from the main serving tables so early-comers can nibble while the rest of the crowd gathers.

Smoked Salmon Canapés

Whether it's a casual get-together or special celebration, these canapés will be a hit!

1 c. sour cream
¼ t. lemon zest
1 loaf party-size light rye bread, crusts removed
¼ c. butter, melted
½ lb. smoked salmon, sliced and cut into ¼-inch strips
Garnish: 2 green onions, thinly sliced

Combine sour cream and lemon zest in a bowl and chill 2 hours. Brush bread slices with butter and cut each slice in half diagonally. Arrange bread triangles on ungreased baking sheets and bake at 350 degrees for about 10 minutes or until lightly toasted. Let cool completely.

Spoon chilled lemon cream on top of each toast. Place a salmon strip on top of toast and garnish with sliced green onions. Makes 5 to 6 dozen.

Crab-Stuffed Mushrooms

You don't have to spend the whole day in the kitchen to make these savory morsels. They are ready to bake in 15 minutes. Make ahead, cover and refrigerate before a party. Add a few minutes to the bake time until they are thoroughly heated and golden.

15 large mushrooms, stems
    removed and reserved
2 T. butter, divided
⅓ c. onion, chopped
¾ t. seafood seasoning
¼ t. salt
¼ t. pepper

6-oz. can crabmeat, drained
1 egg, beaten
½ slice firm white bread,
    crumbled
¼ c. grated Parmesan cheese,
    divided

"Your friends will think you spent the whole day in the kitchen!"

Cindy

    Chop mushroom stems. Butter a 13"x9" baking pan using one tablespoon butter. Place mushroom caps in prepared pan.

    Melt remaining butter in a large skillet over medium heat. Add chopped stems, onion, seafood seasoning, salt and pepper; cook, stirring often, 5 minutes or until tender.

    Combine crabmeat, egg and bread crumbs in a large bowl, stirring well. Add mushroom mixture and 2 tablespoons cheese, stirring well. Spoon filling evenly into mushroom caps; sprinkle with remaining cheese. Bake at 350 degrees for 20 minutes or until golden. Serves 15.

Suzanne Erickson
Columbus, OH

Butterscotch Haystacks

These sweets are a great stand-alone treat or scrumptious with ice cream sandwiched between them.

2 (6-oz.) pkgs. butterscotch chips   3-oz. can chow mein noodles
1 c. cocktail peanuts

Melt butterscotch chips in a heavy saucepan over low heat; stir in peanuts and noodles. Remove from heat; drop by teaspoonfuls onto wax paper. Cool until firm. Makes 18.

Tammy Asbill
Whitehouse, TX

Chocolate-Cherry Crunch

Add a sprinkling of coconut for a tropical taste!

2 (14½-oz.) cans cherry pie filling   1 c. quick-cooking oats,
19.8-oz. pkg. fudge brownie mix   uncooked
½ c. chopped pecans   ¾ c. butter or margarine, melted

Pour pie filling in the bottom of an ungreased 13"x9" baking pan; set aside.

Blend together brownie mix and remaining 3 ingredients in a bowl until coarse crumbs form; sprinkle over pie filling. Bake at 350 degrees for 30 minutes. Makes 12 servings.

Kathy Glass
Neosho, MO

Praline Graham Crackers

With only 4 ingredients, these cookies make a wonderful gift, and they're ready in less than 30 minutes!

1 sleeve graham crackers
1 c. butter

1½ c. brown sugar, packed
2 c. pecans

Arrange a single layer of graham crackers in an ungreased 15"x10" baking pan; set aside.

Bring butter, sugar and pecans to a boil in a heavy saucepan, stirring constantly. Pour over graham crackers; bake at 350 degrees for 10 minutes. Break into pieces to serve. Makes about 30 servings.

Jennifer Eveland-Kupp
Reading, PA

festive invitations

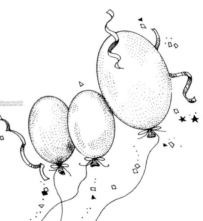

Fill bouquets of balloons with helium and write the who, what, when and where party information on each with a permanent pen. Hand-deliver or tie them securely to doorknobs with lengths of curling ribbon.

Marshmallow Pops

Keep a variety of candy sprinkles on hand for this super quick & easy lunchbox or after-school treat!

10-oz. pkg. marshmallows
12 white craft sticks
12-oz. pkg. semi-sweet
   chocolate chips

2 T. shortening
Garnishes: candy sprinkles,
   toasted coconut, chopped
   nuts

Thread 2 marshmallows on each craft stick; set aside. Melt chocolate chips and shortening in a heavy saucepan over low heat, stirring constantly. Dip marshmallows into chocolate; sprinkle with favorite garnish. Cool on wax paper; store in refrigerator. Makes one dozen.

Judi Gause
Jacksonville Beach, FL

Apple-Cranberry Popsicles

Little ones can't get enough of these fruity popsicles. Keep plenty around for hot summer days.

2 c. plain yogurt
2 t. vanilla extract
12-oz. can unsweetened frozen
    apple cranberry juice
    concentrate, thawed

6 small paper cups
6 plastic spoons

Mix together first 3 ingredients; pour into small paper cups. Insert a plastic spoon into the center of each yogurt cup; freeze overnight. Makes 6.

Jennifer Kirk
Bremerton, WA

Popcorn Bars

Made with popcorn, marshmallows and chocolate, this treat is a winner for sleepovers and kids' parties.

⅔ c. popcorn, unpopped
½ c. butter or margarine
½ c. oil
2 (10½-oz.) pkgs. mini
    marshmallows

2 c. salted peanuts
12-oz. pkg. candy-coated
    chocolate mini-baking bits

Pop the popcorn; remove and discard any unpopped kernels. Set popcorn aside.

Melt butter, oil and marshmallows in a large saucepan over low heat. Stir popcorn into marshmallow mixture; fold in peanuts and baking bits.

Place mixture in 2 greased jelly-roll pans. Cool; cut into squares and serve. Makes 42.

Jen Sell
Farmington, MN

Kiddies' Favorite Trail Mix

This trail mix has something for everyone's tastes...salty, sweet and fruity.

4 c. bite-size crispy corn cereal
    squares
1 c. peanuts

1 c. raisins
½ c. dried bananas, chopped
1 c. candy-coated chocolates

    Stir together all ingredients in a large covered container. Makes about 7½ cups.

Marian Buckley
Fontana, CA

"You'll want to pack these treats in snack-size plastic zipping bags...they're handy for family road trips and quieting cries of 'Are we there yet?'"

Marian

whimsical servers

New plastic pails make whimsical picnic servers for chips and snacks. After lunch, the kids can use them for treasure hunting around the picnic grounds.

Cookie Dough Cheese Ball

This is a hit with kids of all ages. Try dipping graham crackers, animal crackers and even chocolate chip cookies in this special treat.

8-oz. pkg. cream cheese,
   softened
½ c. butter, softened
¼ t. vanilla extract
½ c. powdered sugar

3 T. brown sugar, packed
1 c. mini semi-sweet
   chocolate chips
1 c. pecans, finely chopped

Blend together first 3 ingredients until creamy; add powdered sugar and brown sugar, blending well. Fold in chocolate chips; cover and refrigerate 3 to 4 hours.

Shape dough into a ball; wrap in plastic wrap and refrigerate until firm. Roll in pecans before serving. Makes about 3 cups.

Kristie Rigo
Friedens, PA

Chicken & Dumplin' Soup,
page 57

5 ingredients
or less

With just 5 ingredients or less, great-tasting food is a snap to prepare...and most ingredients are readily found in the kitchen. You'll find an appetizer with 3 ingredients and biscuits made with only 4. For dinner, Oven-Baked Chicken Fingers (page 67) call for 5 ingredients and don't miss the 2-ingredient Orange Sherbet Ice Cream (page 81)! Cooking just got easier!

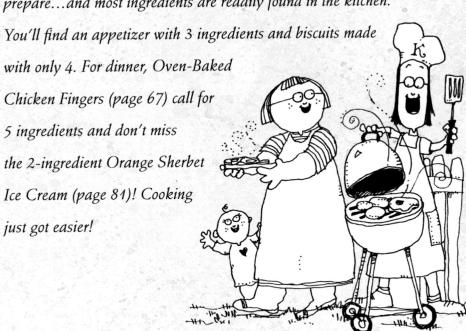

Avocado Dip

The buttery texture and mild, nutlike flavor of an avocado is hard to beat. To make sure your avocados are ripened for this dip, test to see if they yield to gentle pressure. Also, try to flick off the small stem; if it comes off easily and you see green underneath, the avocado is ripe and ready to eat. To ripen a hard avocado, simply place in a paper bag and leave at room temperature; it'll soften in 2 to 5 days.

"This dip is yummy with toasted pita triangles or bagel chips."

Susie

2 avocados, peeled, pitted and chopped
8-oz. pkg. cream cheese, softened

¼ c. mayonnaise
½ to 1 t. garlic salt

Blend together all ingredients; cover and chill until ready to serve. Makes about 2 cups.

Susie Rogers
Puyallup, WA

State Fair Hot Sausage Balls

These sausage balls are equally good served for breakfast or as an appetizer. Feel free to substitute a mild-flavored sausage, if you prefer.

1 lb. ground hot sausage
2 c. biscuit baking mix

10-oz. pkg. shredded sharp Cheddar cheese

Mix together all ingredients; shape into one-inch balls. Arrange on a lightly greased 13"x9" baking sheet; bake at 375 degrees for 18 minutes. Serve warm. Makes 1½ to 2 dozen.

Mary Henson
Eaton, OH

BLT Dip

With all the makings of the popular sandwich, this dip is sure to please.

1 lb. bacon, crisply cooked and
   crumbled
1 c. mayonnaise

1 c. sour cream
2 tomatoes, chopped

Blend together bacon, mayonnaise and sour cream in a medium serving bowl. Add tomatoes just before serving. Makes 2½ cups.

Barbara Thurman
Carlyle, IL

easy chopping

Save time by putting the food processor to work chopping and dicing veggies…so easy!

Texas Caviar

This dip is a hands-down crowd pleaser. Serve it with your favorite multi-colored tortilla chips.

15-oz. can black beans, drained
    and rinsed
15-oz. can black-eyed peas,
    drained and rinsed

15¼-oz. can corn, drained
16-oz. jar salsa
Garnish: chopped fresh cilantro

Stir together all ingredients except cilantro; pour into an airtight container. Refrigerate several hours before serving. Garnish, if desired. Makes 4 cups.

Kathy Wood
La Crescenta, CA

Bits of Sunshine Biscuits

Four ingredients are all it takes to make up a batch of these melt-in-your-mouth bite-size biscuits.

1 c. butter or margarine, melted
8-oz. pkg. shredded sharp
    Cheddar cheese

1 c. sour cream
2 c. self-rising flour

Combine butter and cheese; set aside to cool 2 minutes. Add sour cream; stir in flour. Fill greased mini muffin tins ⅔ full; bake at 350 degrees for 20 to 25 minutes. Makes about 4 dozen.

Donna Bowles
Plant City, FL

easy how-to

Making biscuits and there's no biscuit cutter handy? Try Mom's little trick…just grab a glass tumbler or the open end of a clean, empty soup can.

Mini Dinner Rolls

This batter keeps in the refrigerator for up to 7 days when stored in an airtight container...just bake as needed.

2 c. water
1 pkg. active dry yeast
¾ c. oil

4 c. self-rising flour
¼ c. sugar

Heat water until warm (100 to 110 degrees). Dissolve yeast in warm water in a large bowl; set aside 5 to 10 minutes or until foamy. Add oil and remaining ingredients; mix well. Fill greased or paper-lined mini muffin tins ¾ full; bake at 400 degrees for 15 minutes. Makes 3 to 4 dozen.

Carol Thomson
Abilene, TX

Grape Salad

Add a punch of color to this salad by using red and green seedless grapes.

1 c. brown sugar, packed
1 c. sour cream
1 t. almond extract

1 c. chopped pecans
2 c. seedless grapes, halved

"Sprinkle with cinnamon and sugar, if you'd like."

Cindy

Combine first 3 ingredients; fold in pecans and grapes, mixing gently until well coated. Cover and refrigerate until ready to serve. Makes 4 to 6 servings.

Cindy Calvert
Lubbock, TX

Mozzarella & Tomato Salad

Mozzarella & Tomato Salad

Celebrate summer with fresh-from-the-garden flavors of tomatoes and basil.

8 tomatoes, chopped
(about 3½ lbs.)
½ c. olive oil
pepper to taste

16-oz. pkg. shredded mozzarella
cheese
1 c. fresh basil, torn

Combine all ingredients in a large serving bowl; toss to coat. Cover and refrigerate for 30 minutes before serving. Makes 8 servings.

Zoe Bennett
Columbia, SC

Broccoli-Cauliflower Salad

Broccoli and cauliflower get dressed up with toppings of bacon and cheese.

1 head cauliflower, finely
chopped
1 bunch broccoli, finely chopped

4-oz. jar bacon bits
2 c. shredded Cheddar cheese
8-oz. bottle slaw dressing

Combine cauliflower, broccoli, bacon and cheese; pour dressing over the top. Toss to coat; chill. Serves 10.

Susie Backus
Gooseberry Patch

Crunchy Corn Chip Salad

This recipe easily doubles…or triples for large gatherings.

11-oz. can sweet corn and
    diced peppers, drained
⅓ c. green pepper, minced
¼ c. green onions, chopped

10-oz. pkg. regular-size corn
    chips
8-oz. bottle ranch salad dressing

Combine corn, green pepper and onions in a large serving bowl; refrigerate until ready to serve. Add corn chips and enough ranch dressing to coat salad. Serve immediately. Makes 6 servings.

Linda Bethel
Shidler, OK

potluck favorites

Why not choose comfort foods as the theme of your next school or church potluck? What fun to try everyone's favorite comfort food…and everything is sure to be scrumptious!

Chicken & Dumplin' Soup

(pictured on page 46)

Refrigerated biscuits make this ultimate comfort food ever so easy!

10¾-oz. can cream of chicken
  soup
4 c. chicken broth
4 boneless, skinless chicken
  breasts, cooked and shredded

2 (15-oz.) cans mixed vegetables
12-oz. tube refrigerated biscuits,
  quartered
Optional: pepper to taste

Combine soup and broth in a 6-quart stockpot; bring to a boil over medium-high heat, whisking until smooth. Stir in chicken and vegetables; bring to a boil. Drop biscuit quarters into soup; cover and simmer 15 minutes. Let soup sit 10 minutes before serving. Sprinkle each serving with pepper, if desired. Serves 6 to 8.

Brenda Hancock
Hartford, KY

Vegetable-Cheese Chowder

Keep a package of frozen vegetables in the freezer and cheese in the fridge to whip up a quick lunch or light dinner. For variety, use Swiss or smoked Gouda cheese for the regular Gouda cheese in this recipe.

16-oz. pkg. frozen broccoli,
  cauliflower and carrot mix
2 c. milk, divided

⅓ c. all-purpose flour
14½-oz. can chicken broth
1 c. Gouda cheese, shredded

Prepare vegetables according to package directions; do not drain.
Whisk together ⅔ cup milk and flour; mix well. Pour into vegetables; stir in remaining milk and chicken broth. Cook over medium-high heat, stirring often, until thickened and bubbly; cook one more minute. Reduce heat to low; stir in cheese until melted. Makes 4 servings.

Kathy Grashoff
Fort Wayne, IN

Easy Italian Wedding Soup

Though you probably won't see this recipe on the menu at many weddings, it is a traditional Italian soup that's often served for holidays and other special events.

2 (14½-oz.) cans chicken broth
1 c. water
1 c. medium shell pasta,
   uncooked

16 frozen meatballs, cooked
2 c. spinach leaves, finely
   shredded
1 cup pizza sauce

"We sprinkle each serving with grated Parmesan cheese."

Debby

Bring broth and one cup water to a boil in a large saucepan; add pasta and meatballs. Return to a boil; cook 7 to 9 minutes or until pasta is done. Do not drain. Reduce heat; stir in spinach and pizza sauce. Cook one to 2 minutes or until thoroughly heated. Makes 4 servings.

Debby Horton
Cincinnati, OH

perfect pasta

So many favorite comfort-food recipes begin with pasta or noodles. The secret to perfectly cooked pasta is to use plenty of cooking water…about a gallon per pound of pasta in a very large pot.

Microwave Applesauce

Select tart, juicy all-purpose apples when making this recipe. Some of our favorites are Cortland, Empire, Granny Smith and McIntosh.

6 apples, cored, peeled and
   chopped
¼ c. water

⅓ c. sugar
½ t. cinnamon
¼ t. ground nutmeg

Combine all ingredients in a 2-quart microwave-safe dish. Microwave on high 6 to 8 minutes; transfer to a food processor and process until smooth. Makes 6 to 8 servings.

Tami Bowman
Gooseberry Patch

Mom's Fried Corn

Nothing beats the taste of fresh corn! But if it's not available, feel free to substitute 3 cups of frozen corn kernels.

6 ears corn, husked
1 T. bacon drippings
2 c. water

1 T. butter
salt to taste

Delightful Deviled Eggs

The best method for boiling eggs is to place them in a single layer in a saucepan and add enough water to cover one inch above the eggs. Bring water to a boil; immediately cover pan and remove from heat. Let eggs sit, covered, 15 minutes. Drain the water and immediately place eggs under cold running water.

12 eggs, hard-boiled and peeled
½ c. Thousand Island salad
   dressing

salt and pepper to taste
Garnish: paprika

Slice eggs in half lengthwise. Place yolks in a small mixing bowl and set egg white halves aside.

Mix dressing with egg yolks; add salt and pepper to taste. Spoon mixture into egg white halves. Sprinkle with paprika, if desired. Makes 2 dozen.

Robin Wilson
Altamonte Springs, FL

"My family always looks forward to my special deviled eggs...especially at the holidays."

Robin

Parmesan Noodles

This easy side is a nice complement to chicken, pork or beef. It also serves as a simple one-dish alternative to mac & cheese for the little ones in your family...without the green onions.

8-oz. pkg. medium egg noodles,
   cooked
3 T. green onions, chopped

2 T. butter
½ c. grated Parmesan cheese
garlic salt and pepper to taste

Toss together all ingredients in a serving bowl; serve warm or cold. Makes 4 to 6 servings.

Laura Carman
Hooper, UT

Zucchini Fritters

Zucchini Fritters

Here's a tasty way to get your family to eat their vegetables and use the surplus zucchini from your garden!

2 zucchini, grated (about 3½ c.)
1 egg
⅔ c. shredded Cheddar cheese
⅔ c. round buttery crackers,
    crumbled

Optional: ½ t. seasoned salt
2 T. oil

Combine zucchini, egg, cheese, crackers and, if desired, salt in a large mixing bowl. If mixture seems wet, add extra crackers; shape mixture into patties. Heat oil in a skillet; fry patties about 3 minutes on each side or until golden brown. Makes 4 servings.

Melissa Hart
Middleville, MI

Citrus-Apple Sweet Potatoes

Whole sweet potatoes can be cooked in the microwave like regular baking potatoes. For this recipe, pierce the potatoes several times with a fork. Microwave, uncovered, on high 20 minutes, turning potatoes after 10 minutes. Once they're cooked, submerge the potatoes in cold water...the peels will be easier to remove.

6 sweet potatoes, cooked,
    peeled and mashed
2 c. applesauce

½ c. brown sugar, packed
¼ c. butter
½ c. orange juice

Mix together all ingredients; place in a lightly buttered 2-quart casserole dish. Bake at 350 degrees for 40 minutes. Serves 8 to 10.

Carolyn Kent
Evant, TX

"Our family loves these potatoes alongside a slice of ham."
Carolyn

Rice & Monterey Jack Casserole

If you have leftover rice from a previous meal, feel free to use it in this recipe.

2 c. sour cream
¾ c. cooked rice
2-oz. can diced green chiles

1 c. shredded Monterey Jack
   cheese

Combine sour cream, rice and chiles; arrange in layers with cheese in an ungreased 1½-quart casserole dish. Bake at 350 degrees for 15 minutes or until heated through. Makes 6 servings.

Michelle Serrano
Ramona, CA

Garlic Angel Hair Pasta

Make this recipe even easier by using prepared minced garlic in a jar; you can find it in the produce department of your grocery store. Generally, ½ teaspoon of prepared minced garlic is equivalent to one clove of garlic.

7 cloves garlic, minced
⅓ c. olive oil
16-oz. pkg. angel hair pasta,
   cooked

1⅓ c. seasoned dry bread crumbs

Sauté garlic in oil in a small skillet over low heat until golden. Pour oil and garlic over pasta; sprinkle with bread crumbs. Mix well; cover and set aside for 2 minutes before serving. Makes 8 servings.

Terry Esposito
Freehold, NJ

Cheeseburger Cups

Cheeseburgers in a cup will delight children of all ages! Prepare them as afternoon snacks or as a clever main dish for supper.

12-oz. tube refrigerated biscuits
catsup and mustard to taste

1 lb. ground beef, browned
1 c. shredded Cheddar cheese

"So tasty, and the kids just love them!"

Elizabeth

Spray muffin cups with non-stick vegetable spray. Roll out biscuits until each is big enough to fit into a muffin cup with enough dough to cover. Place in muffin tins.

Mix together catsup and mustard with ground beef. Fill each biscuit cup with meat mixture. Sprinkle cheese over top. Fold dough over top. Bake at 425 degrees for 10 to 12 minutes or until golden brown. Makes 4 to 6 servings.

Elizabeth Bevill
Helena, GA

Cheesy Fiesta Bake

After baking this south-of-the-border casserole, add flair with additional toppings of shredded lettuce, chopped tomatoes and sour cream.

2 lbs. ground beef, browned
1¼-oz. pkg. taco seasoning mix
2 (8-oz.) tubes refrigerated
  crescent rolls

16-oz. jar pasteurized process
  cheese sauce
4-oz. can diced green chiles

Combine ground beef and taco seasoning mix; set aside.

Unfold one tube of crescent rolls and press dough to cover the bottom of a lightly greased 13"x9" baking dish. Layer beef mixture and cheese sauce on top; sprinkle with green chiles. Unfold remaining tube of crescent rolls and arrange dough on top; bake at 400 degrees for 25 to 30 minutes. Makes 8 servings.

Brittany Trotter-McDowell
Ellsinore, MO

Oven-Baked Chicken Fingers

Heating your baking sheet prior to cooking ensures crispier results for your chicken fingers. Serve them with ranch dressing, barbecue sauce or honey mustard for dipping.

1 c. Italian-flavored dry bread crumbs
2 T. grated Parmesan cheese
1 clove garlic, minced

¼ c. oil
6 boneless, skinless chicken breasts

Preheat oven to 425 degrees. Heat a large baking sheet in the oven for 5 minutes.

Combine bread crumbs and cheese in a shallow dish; set aside. Combine garlic and oil in a small bowl; set aside.

Place chicken between 2 sheets of heavy-duty plastic wrap. Flatten chicken to ½-inch thickness, using a meat mallet or rolling pin; cut into one-inch-wide strips. Dip strips in oil mixture; coat with crumb mixture. Coat preheated baking sheet with non-stick vegetable spray and place chicken on prepared baking sheet. Bake at 425 degrees for 12 to 14 minutes, turning after 10 minutes. Serves 6.

Kathy Wood
La Crescenta, CA

Pecan Chicken

Use your food processor to grind the pecans for this recipe.

4 boneless, skinless chicken
   breasts
2 T. honey

2 T. Dijon mustard
2 T. ground pecans

    Place chicken between 2 sheets of heavy-duty plastic wrap. Flatten to ¼-inch thickness, using a meat mallet or rolling pin; set aside.
    Mix together honey and mustard; spread over chicken. Coat chicken with pecans; arrange in a lightly greased 13"x9" baking pan. Bake at 350 degrees for 15 to 18 minutes. Makes 4 servings.

Linda Wiist
Duluth, GA

Ham & Pineapple Kabobs

Remember to boil marinade for one minute before using it as a basting sauce.

1½ lbs. smoked ham, cut into
   one-inch cubes
8-oz. can pineapple chunks,
   juice reserved

6 (6-inch) metal skewers
2 T. soy sauce
2 T. brown sugar, packed

    Thread ham and pineapple alternately onto skewers; place in a 2-quart casserole dish. Combine reserved pineapple juice, soy sauce and brown sugar; pour over kabobs. Cover and marinate in refrigerator 2 hours, turning occasionally. Place marinade in a saucepan; bring to a boil and boil for one minute. Grill kabobs over medium-high heat (350 to 400 degrees) about 10 minutes or until golden, turning twice and brushing with marinade. Makes 3 servings.
    Note: You can also use cored fresh pineapple. Cut it into one-inch pieces and use the juice from the container for your marinade.

Stephanie Moon
Nampa, ID

Toasted Ravioli

We can't decide whether we like this as a crunchy snack or savory side dish. Either way you choose, it's a toasty delight.

25-oz. pkg. frozen ravioli
1 c. dry bread crumbs
¼ c. grated Parmesan cheese

1 egg, beaten
¼ c. milk

Prepare ravioli according to package directions; drain.

Combine bread crumbs and Parmesan cheese in a pie plate; set aside. Whisk together egg and milk; set aside.

Dip ravioli in egg mixture; coat with bread crumb mixture. Sauté in a skillet over medium-high heat until golden, adding one tablespoon olive oil if necessary; drain. Serves 4.

Fran Hynek
Bellevue, NE

Cheesy Pasta Pie

For extra cheesy goodness, sprinkle with shredded mozzarella during the last 5 minutes of baking.

3 c. cooked pasta
2 T. butter, melted
½ c. grated Parmesan cheese,
    divided

1¼ c. spaghetti sauce
1 t. dried oregano

Combine pasta, butter and ¼ cup Parmesan cheese; spread in a lightly greased 10" glass pie plate. Pour spaghetti sauce over the top; sprinkle with oregano and remaining Parmesan cheese. Bake at 350 degrees for 30 minutes. Makes 8 servings.

Marilyn Engelker
Wood River, NE

Ravioli Casserole

Ravioli Casserole

Give frozen ravioli a flavor boost with extra spaghetti sauce and layers of 3 different cheeses. Once your family tastes this ravioli, there will be no more requests for the canned variety!

26-oz. jar spaghetti sauce, divided
25-oz. pkg. frozen cheese ravioli, cooked and divided
2 c. cottage cheese, divided
4 c. shredded mozzarella cheese, divided
¼ c. grated Parmesan cheese

Spread ½ cup spaghetti sauce in a lightly greased 13"x9" baking dish; layer with half the ravioli. Pour 1¼ cups sauce over ravioli; top with one cup cottage cheese and 2 cups mozzarella cheese. Repeat layers; sprinkle with Parmesan cheese. Bake, uncovered, at 350 degrees for 40 minutes. Let stand 10 minutes before serving. Serves 6 to 8.

Donna Nowicki
Center City, MN

Pizza Mac & Cheese

Two favorites, pizza and mac & cheese, in one dish! It's a meal that'll satisfy everyone's cravings.

7¼-oz. pkg. macaroni and cheese
2 eggs, beaten
16-oz. jar pizza sauce
4-oz. pkg. sliced pepperoni
1 c. shredded mozzarella cheese

Prepare macaroni and cheese according to package directions; remove from heat. Add eggs; mix well. Pour into a greased 13"x9" baking pan; bake at 370 degrees for 10 minutes.

Spread pizza sauce over macaroni and cheese; layer pepperoni and mozzarella cheese on top. Bake about 10 more minutes or until cheese melts. Makes 8 servings.

Jesse Ireland
St. Augustine, FL

Sloppy Joe Casserole

Round out this speedy one-dish meal with a salad, and your dinner is complete!

1 lb. ground beef, browned
2 potatoes, sliced

1 onion, chopped
15-oz. can sloppy Joe sauce

Layer ground beef in a 12" skillet; arrange potatoes on top. Sprinkle with onion. Pour sloppy Joe sauce over the mixture; simmer, covered, 30 minutes. Makes 6 to 8 servings.

Louise Fish
Shoreline, WA

Turkey Shepherd's Pie

American cheese and ground turkey give a modern twist to a traditional English dish.

"Quick, easy and scrumptious!"

Leah

1 lb. ground turkey
1 onion, chopped
2 c. brown gravy

8 slices American cheese
4 c. mashed potatoes

Brown ground turkey and onion in a large skillet over medium-high heat, stirring until meat crumbles and is no longer pink; drain.

Place turkey mixture in a greased 2-quart casserole dish. Pour gravy over turkey; top with cheese and mashed potatoes. Bake at 350 degrees for 20 minutes or until hot and bubbly. Makes 4 servings.

Leah Wicker
Chattanooga, TN

You-Name-It Cookies

Keep 'em guessing which flavor they'll bite into when it's your turn to bring dessert. Maybe they should be called Surprise Cookies!

18.25-oz. pkg. favorite-flavor
  cake mix
1 egg, beaten

8-oz. container frozen whipped
  topping, thawed
2 to 3 c. powdered sugar

Combine cake mix and egg; blend in whipped topping. Drop by teaspoonfuls into powdered sugar; coat completely. Place on ungreased baking sheets; bake at 350 degrees for 8 to 10 minutes. Cool on baking sheets. Makes 3 dozen.

Suzanne Killmon
Wallops Island, VA

"Whoever chooses the cake mix flavor gets to name the cookies. We might have Sis's Strawberry Sweeties or Ma's Mega Lemon Snappers."

Suzanne

just-right cookies

Keep crisp cookies crisp and soft cookies soft in a cookie jar or tin…separate the layers with sheets of wax paper.

Soft Peanut Butter Cookies

Soft Peanut Butter Cookies

If you're a peanut butter fan, these cookies won't last long. You'll enjoy every last crumb! Don't forget to serve them with a tall, cold glass of milk.

1 c. sugar
1 c. creamy peanut butter

1 egg, slightly beaten
1 t. vanilla extract

Combine all ingredients; mix well. Roll dough into one-inch balls and place on an ungreased baking sheet. Use a fork to press a crisscross pattern into the top of each cookie. Bake at 325 degrees for 10 minutes or until golden. Let cool before removing from sheet. Makes 2 dozen.

Brenda Tranka
Amboy, IL

"This recipe is from my late sister. She loved to write down recipes... I framed several of them to remember her by."

Brenda

S'more Bars

Chopped pecans are added to this version of the favorite campfire treat... and you get to enjoy them in the comfort of your own home!

8 to 10 whole graham crackers
20-oz. pkg. brownie mix
2 c. mini marshmallows

1 c. semi-sweet chocolate chips
⅔ c. chopped pecans

Arrange graham crackers in a single layer in a greased 13"x9" baking pan; set aside. Prepare brownie mix according to package directions (do not bake); carefully spread over graham crackers.

Bake at 350 degrees for 25 to 30 minutes. Sprinkle marshmallows, chocolate chips and pecans over brownie layer; bake 5 more minutes or until golden. Cut into bars when cool. Makes 2 dozen.

Jo Ann
Gooseberry Patch

"All the campfire flavor of s'mores... enjoy them anytime!"

Jo Ann

Microwave Peanut Toffee

No candy thermometer is needed for this quick toffee!

¾ c. finely chopped unsalted
   peanuts, divided
½ c. butter
1 c. sugar

¼ c. water
1 c. peanut butter-and-milk
   chocolate chips

Spread ½ cup chopped peanuts into a 9-inch circle on a lightly greased baking sheet. Coat top 2 inches of a 2½-quart microwave-safe glass bowl with butter; place remaining butter in bowl. Add sugar and ¼ cup water to bowl. (Do not stir.) Microwave on high 8 minutes or just until mixture begins to turn light brown; carefully pour over peanuts on baking sheet. Sprinkle with chips; let stand one minute. Spread melted chips evenly over peanut mixture and sprinkle with remaining chopped peanuts. Chill until firm. Break into bite-size pieces. Store in an airtight container. Makes one pound.

Note: This recipe was tested in an 1100-watt microwave oven.

Yummy Chocolate Crunch

Saltine crackers serve as the base of this simple chocolate treat.

"So easy to bring along to parties or even into work."

Rebecca

1 sleeve saltine crackers
1 c. sugar

1 c. butter
12-oz. pkg. chocolate chips

Place crackers, side by side, in a 13"x9" baking dish lined with aluminum foil until bottom of dish is covered. Bring sugar and butter to a boil in a saucepan; boil 3 minutes, stirring constantly. Pour mixture over crackers and spread with a spatula until crackers are covered.

Bake at 350 degrees for 10 to 15 minutes or until edges of crackers are golden brown. Immediately remove from oven; spread chocolate chips evenly over crackers until chocolate is melted. Freeze 2 hours. Break into pieces. Makes 12 to 14 servings.

Rebecca Santelli
Mechanicsville, VA

Easy Vanilla Fudge

Stir in sweetened, dried cranberries for a touch of color...and added flavor.

8-oz. pkg. cream cheese, softened
4 c. powdered sugar
1½ t. vanilla extract
12-oz. pkg. white chocolate chips
¾ c. chopped nuts

Blend together cream cheese, powdered sugar and vanilla until smooth and creamy; set aside.

Melt chips in a heavy saucepan over low heat; stir into cream cheese mixture, mixing well. Fold in nuts; pour into a lightly buttered 8"x8" baking pan. Refrigerate until firm; cut into squares to serve. Makes 4 dozen servings.

Connie Frey
Palmerton, PA

Chocolate-Peanut Butter Squares

Chocolate and peanut butter are a winning combination every time!

18.25-oz. pkg. chocolate fudge cake mix with pudding
½ c. oil
2 eggs
6-oz. pkg. peanut butter chips

Mix together dry cake mix, oil and eggs; stir in peanut butter chips. Spread in a greased 13"x9" baking pan. Bake at 350 degrees for 8 minutes. Let cool; cut into 2-inch squares. Makes 3 dozen.

Rita Brooks
Norman, OK

"A really fast, tasty recipe...I use it all the time in a pinch!"

Rita

Magic Bars

You've probably seen many variations of this recipe and each is as wonderful as the other. So put together some magic of your own with this tasty treat.

½ c. butter or margarine, melted
1⅓ c. graham cracker crumbs
14-oz. can sweetened condensed milk

1½ c. semi-sweet chocolate chips
1½ c. chopped walnuts

Stir together butter and graham cracker crumbs; press into a 13"x9" baking dish. Pour milk over crumb mixture; sprinkle with chocolate chips and walnuts. Bake at 350 degrees for 25 minutes or until edges are browned and bubbly. Makes 2 dozen.

Melanie Heffner
Beaverton, OR

"As fast as my Auntie Jo bakes 'em...they disappear!"

Melanie

breezy clean-up

Line your brownie dish with aluminum foil...be sure to grease. After brownies are baked and cooled, they lift right out. And best of all, clean-up is a breeze!

Chocolate Picnic Cake

A whole package of chocolate chips is stirred into this easy cake that starts with a mix.

18.25-oz. pkg. chocolate
    cake mix
1 T. all-purpose flour

6-oz. pkg. chocolate chips
Garnish: powdered sugar

Mix cake according to package directions; stir in flour. Pour mixture into a greased 13"x9" baking pan; sprinkle with chocolate chips.

Bake cake according to package directions. Let cool in pan; when cool, sprinkle with powdered sugar, if desired. Cut into squares. Makes 12 to 15 servings.

Jo Anne Hayon
Sheboygan, WI

Easy Key Lime Pie

Convenience products add to the simplicity of this frozen citrus pie.

6-oz. can frozen limeade
    concentrate, thawed
14-oz. can sweetened condensed
    milk

9-oz. container frozen whipped
    topping, thawed
9-inch graham cracker pie crust

Combine limeade, milk and whipped topping in a large mixing bowl; mix well. Pour into pie crust; freeze 3 to 4 hours or until firm. Serves 8.

Paula Eggleston
Knoxville, TN

Chocolate Chip Cookie Dough Pie

The crust of this pie is made of chocolate chip cookie dough!

18-oz. tube refrigerated
    chocolate chip cookie dough
2 (8-oz.) pkgs. cream cheese
2 eggs

½ c. sugar
5 (6-oz.) chocolate-covered
    toffee candy bars, crushed

Press cookie dough into an ungreased 9" pie plate. Combine cream cheese and remaining 3 ingredients and pour over top of cookie dough.

Bake, uncovered, at 325 degrees for 30 to 35 minutes. Refrigerate immediately until ready to serve. Makes 8 servings.

Kay Bissell
Taylor, AR

"There is nothing better than chocolate chip cookie dough!"

Kay

Orange Sherbet Ice Cream

It's true! Two ingredients are all it takes to make this creamy sherbet... and one of the ingredients is orange soda.

14-oz. can sweetened condensed
    milk

2 ltrs. orange soda

Combine milk and soda; add to ice cream maker. Freeze according to manufacturer's instructions. Makes about 2 quarts.

Debbie Crawford
Strafford, MO

Super Cranberry Sauce

Cranberries are not just for the holiday season…this sauce is tasty all year 'round! Serve it warm over your favorite dessert.

1 c. orange juice
2 c. sugar

3 c. cranberries

Combine all ingredients in a large saucepan. Cook over medium heat, stirring constantly, until berries burst. Makes about 3 cups.

Karen Uyeda
San Jose, CA

Caramel Sauce

A touch of ground cinnamon is added to this caramel sauce. Serve it over pound cake, shortbread or ice cream.

1 c. brown sugar, packed
½ c. whipping cream
¼ c. corn syrup

1 T. butter
2 t. cinnamon

Combine all ingredients in a saucepan; bring to a boil, stirring constantly. Reduce heat and simmer, uncovered, about 5 minutes. Makes 1½ cups.

Sarina Quaderer
Friendship, WI

German Apple Pancake,
page 110

breakfast
for dinner

Breakfast is touted as the best way to begin your day…so why
not end your day with breakfast, too? Breakfast foods are
generally not fussy or complicated to assemble…perfect for those
busy weeknights. With selections like
Jump-Start Pizza (page 91) and
Savory Stuffed French Toast
(page 106) to choose from, these
recipes are a definite happy
way to end the day.

Baked Garden Omelet

Chock-full of vegetables, this is one omelet you don't have to flip! It's baked in a casserole dish.

8 eggs, beaten
1 c. ricotta cheese
½ c. milk
½ t. dried basil
¼ t. salt
¼ t. fennel seed, crushed
¼ t. pepper

10-oz. pkg. frozen spinach, thawed and drained
1 c. tomatoes, chopped
1 c. shredded mozzarella cheese
½ c. green onions, sliced
½ c. salami, diced

Whisk together eggs and ricotta cheese in a large mixing bowl; add milk, basil, salt, fennel seed and pepper. Fold in spinach and remaining ingredients; spread in a greased 13"x9" baking pan.

Bake at 325 degrees for 30 to 35 minutes or until a toothpick inserted in center comes out clean; let stand 10 minutes before serving. Serves 6 to 8.

Kathy Unruh
Fresno, CA

morning cheer

Tuck cheery blossoms inside lots of 1950's-era egg cups and scatter them on the breakfast table. They'll make everyone feel perky even before the orange juice is served!

Tex-Mex Scramble

Topped with salsa, sour cream and green onions, this festive scramble makes a quick breakfast or dinner.

2 t. oil, divided
3 (6-inch) corn tortillas, cut into
    ½-inch strips
1 small onion, chopped
8 eggs, beaten

½ t. salt
⅛ t. pepper
1 c. salsa
¼ c. sour cream
2 green onions, chopped

Heat 1½ teaspoons oil in a skillet over medium-high heat. Add tortilla strips and cook until crisp. Remove tortilla strips; set aside.

Add remaining ½ teaspoon oil to skillet. Add onion; reduce heat to medium and cook 6 minutes or until onion is tender. Return tortilla strips to skillet; add eggs and stir gently over medium heat until done. Add salt and pepper. Top each serving with salsa, sour cream and green onions. Serves 4.

Kathy Grashoff
Fort Wayne, IN

Ranch House Burritos

Your family will run to the table for these super sausage burritos!

1 lb. ground pork sausage
1 green pepper, chopped
1 onion, diced
6 eggs, beaten

8 (10-inch) flour tortillas,
    warmed
Garnish: picante sauce

Combine first 3 ingredients in a skillet over medium heat; cook until sausage is browned and vegetables are tender. Drain; return to skillet. Stir in eggs; cook until eggs are cooked through. Spoon mixture evenly into tortillas; roll up. Garnish, if desired. Serves 8.

Jason Keller
Carrollton, GA

Simply Scrumptious Frittata

This is a tasty way to use any remaining ham from Sunday dinner...try different cheeses for variety.

1 T. oil
½ c. onion, chopped
½ c. green pepper, chopped
1 to 2 cloves garlic, minced
4 Yukon Gold potatoes, cubed
   and cooked

¾ c. cooked ham, cubed
8 eggs, beaten
salt and pepper to taste
¾ c. shredded Cheddar cheese

Heat oil in a large heavy oven-proof skillet over medium heat. Add onion and green pepper; cook until tender. Add garlic; cook one more minute. Stir in potatoes and ham; cook until heated through. Reduce heat to medium-low; add eggs, salt and pepper. Cook 5 minutes or until eggs are firm on the bottom.

Top eggs with cheese; bake at 350 degrees for 5 to 10 minutes or until cheese melts. Cut into wedges to serve. Serves 4.

Jill Valentine
Jackson, TN

Ham & 2-Cheese Strata

Served with a tossed salad and a fruit cup, this makes an easy dinner for 4.

3 eggs
¼ c. plus 2 T. milk
black pepper to taste
3 slices sourdough bread, halved
1 c. shredded mozzarella cheese
1 c. shredded sharp Cheddar
   cheese

2 green onions, minced
⅓ c. roasted red peppers,
   chopped
4 thin slices cooked ham

Beat together eggs, milk and black pepper in a shallow dish; add bread and let stand 5 minutes.

Layer half of bread slices in the bottom of a lightly greased 9"x5" loaf pan. Top with half each of cheeses, onions, red peppers and ham slices. Pour half of egg mixture over top. Repeat layers, ending with egg mixture. Bake at 350 degrees for 40 minutes or until golden and cheese bubbles. Let cool slightly before serving. Serves 4.

Vickie
Gooseberry Patch

relaxing brunch

If weeknights are busy, why not enjoy a family brunch together on the weekend? Relax with each other over tea & coffee, a basket of muffins and savory Ham & 2-Cheese Strata. You'll be glad you did!

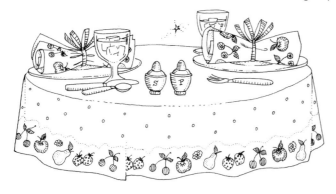

Jump-Start Pizza

Add your own special toppings before baking.

8-oz. tube refrigerated crescent rolls, separated
28-oz. pkg. frozen shredded hashbrowns with onions and peppers, slightly thawed and divided
6 slices bacon, crisply cooked and crumbled
4.5-oz. can diced green chiles, drained
½ to 1 c. shredded Cheddar cheese
5 eggs, beaten

Arrange crescent rolls to cover the bottom of an ungreased pizza pan; press seams together and pinch edges to form a slight rim. Spread half the hashbrowns evenly over the crust, reserving remaining hashbrowns for another recipe; sprinkle with bacon, chiles and cheese. Carefully pour eggs over top; bake at 375 degrees for 30 to 35 minutes. Slice into wedges to serve. Makes 8 servings.

Mari MacLean
Bonita, CA

special touch

Surprise overnight guests by leaving special treats in their room… wrap up fragrant soaps in plush terry washcloths. Leave a few mints on their pillows, or set up a small coffee maker with mugs and individual coffee packets for them to enjoy.

Ham & Egg Casserole

Cubes of ham are combined with a creamy cheese sauce and served over hot baked biscuits for a welcoming meal any time of day.

½ t. onion powder
5 eggs, hard-boiled and chopped
10¾-oz. can cream of chicken
  soup
¼ c. milk

2 c. shredded Cheddar cheese
1 c. cooked ham, cubed
12-oz. tube refrigerated biscuits,
  baked

Combine onion powder, eggs, soup, milk and cheese in a medium mixing bowl; blend well. Place mixture in a greased 8"x8" baking dish. Spread ham evenly over top.

Bake, uncovered, at 350 degrees for 25 minutes. Serve over biscuits. Makes 4 to 6 servings.

Gale Willy
Star City, IN

"This unusual recipe is a favorite at our house. Since we seldom eat a big breakfast, we have it for supper instead."

Gale

Best Brunch Casserole

Croutons are the secret ingredients in this breakfast casserole…giving you a bit of crunch in each bite.

4 c. croutons
2 c. shredded Cheddar cheese
8 eggs, beaten
4 c. milk
1 t. salt

1 t. pepper
2 t. mustard
1 T. dried, minced onion
6 slices bacon, crisply cooked
   and crumbled

Spread croutons in the bottom of a greased 13"x9" baking dish; sprinkle with cheese. Set aside.

Whisk together eggs, milk, salt, pepper, mustard and onion; pour over cheese. Sprinkle bacon on top; bake at 325 degrees for 55 to 60 minutes or until set. Serves 8.

Lita Hardy
Santa Cruz, CA

breakfast in bed

Mom will love breakfast in bed when it's served on a tray filled with special memories. Remove the glass from a serving tray and slide in a piece of card stock that's the same size. Layer on a collage of favorite things…photos, ticket stubs, kids' art or pressed flowers, then gently replace the glass top.

Southern Country Casserole

This casserole earns its Southern title because of the grits stirred into it.

2 c. water
½ c. quick-cooking grits, uncooked
3½ c. shredded Cheddar cheese, divided
4 eggs, beaten
1 c. milk
½ t. salt
½ t. pepper
1 lb. ground sausage, browned
1 T. fresh parsley, chopped

Bring 2 cups water to a boil in a large saucepan; add grits. Return to a boil; reduce heat and simmer 4 minutes. Mix in 2 cups cheese; stir until melted.

Remove saucepan from heat; add eggs, milk, salt, pepper and sausage, mixing well. Pour into a greased 13"x9" baking dish; bake at 350 degrees for 45 to 50 minutes.

Sprinkle with remaining cheese and parsley; return to oven and bake 5 more minutes or until cheese melts. Serves 6 to 8.

Michelle Garner
Tampa, FL

Spinach Squares

These pair easily with any entrée to round out your breakfast…or dinner.

4 c. shredded Cheddar cheese
10-oz. pkg. frozen chopped spinach, thawed
1 c. all-purpose flour
1 t. salt
1 t. baking powder
½ c. onion, chopped

Blend together all ingredients. Spread in a lightly greased 13"x9" baking dish. Bake at 350 degrees for 35 minutes. Let cool slightly; cut into squares. Makes 9 to 12 servings.

Amy Davila
Fowlerville, MI

3-Ingredient Sausage Squares

This recipe can easily be halved and baked in an 8"x8" baking dish.

2 lbs. ground sausage
2 (8-oz.) pkgs. cream cheese,
  softened

2 (8-oz.) tubes refrigerated
  crescent rolls

Brown sausage in a 12" skillet; drain. Add cream cheese, stirring until melted and well blended; remove from heat and set aside.

Press dough from one tube crescent rolls into a greased 13"x9" baking dish, being sure to cover bottom and part of the way up sides of dish; press seams together. Pour sausage mixture over top; set aside. Roll remaining crescent roll dough into a 13"x9" rectangle; layer over sausage mixture.

Bake at 350 degrees for 15 to 20 minutes or until golden; cut into squares to serve. Serves 12.

Shelley Wellington
Dyersburg, TN

plan ahead

Having friends over for breakfast? Set the table the night before...one less thing to think about in the morning!

Golden Home Fries

You can't miss when you pair these fries with your favorite breakfast dish.

3 T. olive oil, divided
1 onion, chopped
1 green pepper, chopped
4 redskin potatoes, cooked and
    cut into ½-inch cubes

¾ t. paprika
1 t. salt
¼ t. pepper
¼ c. fresh parsley, chopped

Heat one tablespoon oil in a large skillet over medium heat. Add onion and green pepper; cook 5 minutes or until tender, stirring often. Remove vegetables from skillet with a slotted spoon; set aside.

Add remaining oil to skillet; increase heat to medium-high. Add potatoes, paprika, salt and pepper; cook 10 minutes or until golden, stirring often. Stir in onion mixture and parsley; cook one more minute, stirring constantly. Serves 4.

Jennifer Patrick
Delaware, OH

Sausage & Egg Muffins

These muffins are all you need to start your morning off right.

1 lb. ground sausage
1 onion, chopped
12 eggs, beaten
2 c. shredded Cheddar cheese

1 t. garlic powder
½ t. salt
½ t. pepper

Brown sausage and onion in a skillet over medium heat; drain. Combine eggs and remaining 4 ingredients in a large mixing bowl. Add sausage mixture; mix well. Spoon into greased muffin cups, filling ⅔ full; bake at 350 degrees for 25 minutes or until a toothpick inserted in center comes out clean. Makes 22.

Rhonda Jones
Rocky Mount, VA

Banana Bread Muffins

A favorite loaf bread is made into muffins…with the addition of chocolate chips! Make sure your bananas are very ripe. You'll want the peels to look very speckled to almost black.

1 c. oil
1 c. sugar
2 eggs, beaten
3 bananas, mashed
1½ c. all-purpose flour

½ c. whole-wheat flour
½ t. salt
2 to 3 T. lemon juice
2 t. baking soda
1 c. semi-sweet chocolate chips

Blend together oil and sugar in a large bowl; add eggs and bananas and set aside.

Mix together flours and salt; stir into oil mixture. Add lemon juice and baking soda; fold in chocolate chips. Spoon into greased muffin cups, filling ⅔ full. Bake at 350 degrees for 25 minutes. Makes about 2 dozen.

Bonnie Fuller
Lead, SD

muffins anytime

Extra muffins can be wrapped in aluminum foil and kept in the freezer for up to a month. To serve, reheat at 300 degrees for 15 to 18 minutes.

Cranberry-Buttermilk Scones

Enjoy these scones fresh from the oven with a dollop of butter or as an afternoon snack with tea…they're a favorite anytime you eat them.

2 c. all-purpose flour
⅓ c. sugar
¼ t. salt
1½ t. baking powder
½ t. baking soda

6 T. butter
⅔ c. sweetened dried cranberries
½ c. buttermilk
1 egg
1½ t. vanilla extract

Stir together first 5 ingredients; cut in butter with a pastry blender. Stir in cranberries. Combine buttermilk, egg and vanilla; mix into flour mixture until just moistened.

Drop dough in 10 tablespoonfuls onto a greased baking sheet. Bake at 375 degrees for 15 minutes or until golden. Makes 10.

Jenny Sisson
Broomfield, CO

soothing tea

A cup of herbal tea is perfect with breakfast recipes or with an afternoon snack. Instead of sweetening a cup of tea with sugar, add one or 2 old-fashioned lemon drops.

Ham & Cheese Muffins

Just add some fruit, and you've got breakfast.

2½ c. biscuit baking mix
¾ c. half-and-half
3 T. oil
1 egg, lightly beaten

¾ c. diced ham
¾ c. shredded sharp Cheddar
    cheese

Pour biscuit mix into a mixing bowl; make a well in center. Combine half-and-half and remaining 4 ingredients; pour into well and stir just until moistened. Spoon into 12 greased muffin cups, filling ⅔ full. Bake at 400 degrees for 11 to 12 minutes or until a toothpick inserted in center comes out clean. Makes one dozen.

Kathy Grashoff
Fort Wayne, IN

Mini Breakfast Cups

All your favorites together…biscuits, sausage and eggs.

"This family favorite is a recipe I often make for church breakfasts. It's a cinch to prepare and bakes in minutes."

Marie

2 (12-oz.) tubes refrigerated
    biscuits
4 to 5 eggs, beaten
1 lb. ground sausage, browned

1 c. shredded Monterey Jack
    cheese
1 c. shredded mild Cheddar
    cheese

Separate each biscuit in half; press into lightly greased mini muffin cups. Cook eggs, without stirring, in a non-stick skillet over medium heat until eggs begin to set on bottom. Draw a spatula across bottom of skillet to form large curds. Continue cooking until eggs are thickened and firm throughout, but still moist. (Do not stir constantly.)

Combine scrambled eggs, sausage and cheeses. Spoon into biscuit halves in muffin cups. Bake at 400 degrees for 7 to 10 minutes or until biscuits are golden around the edges. Makes 3 to 4 dozen.

Marie Stowers
Jacksonville, FL

Cheddar-Apple Biscuits

Apples & cheese are a natural combination, and their flavors are enhanced when baked with brown sugar and cinnamon.

⅓ c. brown sugar, packed
2 T. all-purpose flour
½ t. cinnamon
10-oz. tube refrigerated
    buttermilk biscuits

1 c. shredded Cheddar cheese
2 apples, cored, peeled and sliced
    into rings
1 T. butter, melted

Combine first 3 ingredients in a small bowl; set aside.

Press each biscuit into a 3-inch circle. Place on lightly greased baking sheets; sprinkle each with cheese and top with an apple ring. Sprinkle with sugar mixture and drizzle with melted butter. Bake at 350 degrees for 15 minutes or until crust is golden. Makes 10 servings.

Tammie Jones
Lincolnton, NC

make it special

Cookie cutters make breakfast a treat...use them to cut out biscuit dough, shape pancakes or cut shapes from the center of French toast. Use mini cutters to make the sweetest pats of butter!

Strawberry Cheesecake French Toast

Two favorite foods in one dish…strawberries and cheesecake. Now that's something to wake up to!

4-oz. pkg. cream cheese, softened
2 T. powdered sugar
2 T. strawberry preserves
8 slices country white bread

2 eggs
½ c. half-and-half
2 T. sugar
4 T. butter, divided

Combine cream cheese and powdered sugar in a small bowl; mix well. Stir in preserves. Spread cream cheese mixture evenly over 4 slices of bread; top with remaining slices to form sandwiches. Whisk together eggs, half-and-half and sugar in a medium bowl; set aside.

Melt 2 tablespoons butter in a large skillet over medium heat. Dip each sandwich into egg mixture, completely covering both sides. Cook 2 sandwiches at a time for one to 2 minutes per side or until golden. Melt remaining butter and cook remaining sandwiches as instructed. Serves 4.

Kris Coburn
Dansville, NY

"I like to dress up this dish by topping it with extra powdered sugar, fresh fruit and a drizzle of maple syrup."

Kris

Savory Stuffed French Toast

This toast will satisfy both the sweet & savory folks. It's stuffed with sausage and cheese and then dipped in a cinnamon-sugar mixture before cooking.

8 thick slices French bread
2 T. butter, softened
8-oz. pkg. brown & serve
    sausage patties, browned,
    drained and cut into bite-size
    pieces

1 c. shredded Swiss cheese
2 eggs
½ c. milk
1½ t. sugar
¼ t. cinnamon

Cut a pocket in the crust of each slice of bread; spread butter in each pocket. Set aside.

Combine sausage and cheese; stuff into pockets. Beat together eggs, milk, sugar and cinnamon in a shallow bowl; dip bread into egg mixture. Cook on a greased griddle until both sides are golden, turning once. Serves 4.

Danielle Keeney
Kutztown, PA

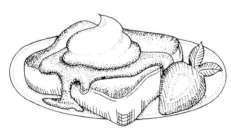

special topping

French toast is scrumptious topped with homemade whipped cream. For the fluffiest whipped cream possible, always make sure the bowl and beaters are chilled.

French Toast Sticks

These French Toast Sticks are easy for little fingers to pick up. Provide applesauce or warm maple syrup for dipping.

4 to 5 slices bread
3 c. crispy rice cereal, crushed
1 T. sugar
1 t. cinnamon
3 eggs, beaten

1 c. milk
1 t. vanilla extract
⅛ t. salt
¼ c. butter, melted

Cut each slice of bread into 4 strips. Combine crushed cereal, sugar and cinnamon in a medium bowl; set aside.

Mix together eggs, milk, vanilla and salt in another bowl. Dip each bread stick into egg mixture and then into sugar coating. Place sticks in an ungreased 13"x9" baking pan; pour melted butter over top. Bake at 375 degrees for 15 to 20 minutes or until golden. Makes 16 to 20 sticks.

Margaret Shelton
Delaware, OH

Monkey Bread

It'll be hard to keep snackers at bay once this caramel-flavored pull-apart bread comes out of the oven.

½ c. sugar
1½ t. cinnamon
3 (12-oz.) tubes refrigerated
   biscuits, quartered

1 c. brown sugar, packed
½ c. butter, melted
2 T. water

Combine sugar and cinnamon in a bowl. Roll biscuit pieces in sugar mixture; place in a greased Bundt® pan. Combine brown sugar, butter and water; pour over biscuits. Bake at 350 degrees for 30 minutes. Invert onto serving plate. Serves 6 to 8.

Michelle Pettit
Sebree, KY

"This is really quick & easy and always a big hit. I usually have to make two because our preacher will try to sneak away with one to take home!"

Michelle

Scrumptious Blueberry Pancakes

Keep pancakes warm & toasty in a 200-degree oven.

1 c. milk
½ c. water
1 c. plus 2 T. whole-wheat flour
½ c. cornmeal
1 t. baking powder
½ t. baking soda
¼ t. salt
1 c. blueberries
2 T. oil, divided
Garnish: jam or syrup

Mix together milk and water in a small bowl; set aside.

Sift together flour, cornmeal, baking powder, baking soda and salt in a large bowl; mix well. Stir in milk mixture just until combined. Fold in blueberries; let stand 5 minutes.

Heat one tablespoon oil in a large skillet over medium heat. Pour ¼ cup batter per pancake into skillet; cook until bubbly on top and edges are slightly dry. Turn and cook other side until golden. Repeat with remaining oil and batter. Serve warm with jam or syrup, if desired. Makes one dozen pancakes.

Jo Ann
Gooseberry Patch

whimsical pancakes

Lightly coat the inside of a cookie cutter with non-stick vegetable spray, then secure it with a clip-on clothespin to the side of the skillet. Pour pancake batter inside the cookie cutter. The clothespin makes it easy to remove the hot cookie cutter from the skillet, resulting in easy, fun-shaped pancakes.

German Apple Pancake
(pictured on page 84)

This is one giant pancake that's cooked with cinnamon-flavored apples, cut into wedges and served with a cream sauce instead of traditional syrup. We used Braeburn apples, but Jonathan or McIntosh apples are also a good choice.

¼ c. butter
1½ t. cinnamon, divided
2 apples, cored, peeled and
    thinly sliced
3 eggs, beaten
½ c. frozen apple juice
    concentrate, thawed

½ c. all-purpose flour
¼ c. half-and-half
1½ t. vanilla extract
¼ t. ground nutmeg
⅛ t. salt
Apple Cream

Melt butter with ½ teaspoon cinnamon over medium heat in a 10" oven-proof skillet. Add apples and sauté 4 minutes or until tender; set aside.

Place remaining 1 teaspoon cinnamon, eggs and next 6 ingredients in a food processor; process until smooth. Pour over apples.

Bake at 450 degrees for 10 minutes or until set. Cut into wedges; place on serving plates. Spoon Apple Cream on top before serving. Makes 6 servings.

Apple Cream:

½ c. plain yogurt
½ t. vanilla extract

2 T. frozen apple juice
    concentrate, thawed

Whisk together all ingredients until smooth.

Marilyn Williams
Westerville, OH

Blueberry Pillows

A blend of cream cheese and blueberries is sandwiched between Italian bread slices in this French toast variation.

8-oz. pkg. cream cheese,
　softened
16 slices Italian bread
½ c. blueberries

2 eggs
½ c. milk
1 t. vanilla extract

Spread cream cheese evenly on 8 bread slices; arrange blueberries evenly over the cream cheese. Top with remaining bread slices, gently pressing together; set aside.

Whisk together eggs, milk and vanilla in a shallow dish; brush over bread slices. Arrange on a hot griddle; cook until golden. Flip and cook other side until golden. Serves 8.

Kristie Rigo
Friedens, PA

year-round fresh blueberries

Enjoy fresh blueberries throughout the year…just freeze them during berry season! Spread ripe berries in a single layer on a baking sheet and freeze until solid, then store them in plastic zipping bags. Later, you can pour out just the amount you need.

Sticky Buns

Welcome guests with the butterscotch aroma and flavor of this tempting sweet bread. These rolls can rise in the refrigerator up to 48 hours. Just let them stand at room temperature until doubled in bulk before baking as directed.

3½-oz. pkg. cook & serve
  butterscotch pudding mix
½ c. brown sugar, packed

1 t. cinnamon
½ c. butter, melted
18 frozen dinner rolls

Combine first 3 ingredients in a large bowl. Stir in butter. Add rolls, stirring to coat. Arrange rolls and pudding mixture in an even layer in a lightly greased 14-cup Bundt® pan. Cover tightly with lightly greased aluminum foil. Let rise at room temperature 8 hours or just until doubled in bulk.

Uncover and bake at 350 degrees for 30 minutes or until golden. Carefully invert rolls onto a serving platter. Serves 12.

Catherine Smith
Champlin, MN

Breakfast Delights

Don't save these buttery, cinnamon-cream cheese treats just for breakfast!
They're also ideal for after-school snacks or for casual gatherings.

2 (8-oz.) pkgs. cream cheese,
   softened
2 c. sugar, divided
1 egg yolk
1 t. vanilla extract

24-oz. loaf sliced white bread,
   crusts trimmed
cinnamon to taste
1 c. butter, melted

Mix together cream cheese, ½ cup sugar, egg yolk and vanilla.
Spread one tablespoon mixture on each bread slice. Roll up bread from
one corner to the other.

Mix together cinnamon and remaining sugar in a shallow bowl.
Dip rolled bread in melted butter, then roll in cinnamon-sugar mixture.

Place rolls on ungreased baking sheets; freeze at least 20 minutes.
Bake at 350 degrees for 8 to 10 minutes or until hot and bubbly. Makes
about 2 dozen.

Marlene Lambie
Camdenton, MO

rise and shine

Weekend sleepyheads love to wake up to the aroma of breakfast in
the air. Before they come to breakfast, make the table look extra
special...daisies tucked in glass milk bottles and a colorful tablecloth
made from vintage-style oilcloth add festive flair.

Go-Bananas Coffee Cake

Friends are sure to "go bananas" over this coffee cake. Cream cheese and cinnamon-sugar pecans add to the flavor of this yummy treat that's perfect for breakfast or anytime!

8-oz. pkg. cream cheese,
   softened
½ c. butter, softened
1¼ c. sugar
2 eggs
3 bananas, mashed

1 t. vanilla extract
2¼ c. all-purpose flour
1½ t. baking powder
½ t. baking soda
Pecan Topping

Blend together cream cheese, butter and sugar until fluffy in a large mixing bowl; add eggs, one at a time, blending well after each addition. Mix in bananas and vanilla; set aside.

Combine flour, baking powder and baking soda; gradually add to creamed mixture, mixing well. Stir in half the Pecan Topping; pour into a greased 13"x9" baking pan. Sprinkle with remaining Pecan Topping; bake at 350 degrees for 25 to 30 minutes. Serves 12.

Pecan Topping:

1 c. chopped pecans
2 T. sugar

1 t. cinnamon

Toss together all ingredients until pecans are well coated.

Sandy Bernards
Valencia, CA

Overnight Coffee Cake

If you decide you just can't wait and want to enjoy this coffee cake right away, skip letting it sit overnight and go ahead and bake as directed... it'll still be moist and delicious.

2 c. all-purpose flour
1 t. baking powder
1 t. baking soda
½ t. salt
1 c. sugar
1 c. brown sugar, packed and
    divided

2 t. cinnamon, divided
1 c. buttermilk
⅔ c. butter, melted
2 eggs
½ c. chopped pecans, toasted

Combine first 5 ingredients, ½ cup brown sugar and one teaspoon cinnamon in a large mixing bowl; add buttermilk, butter and eggs. Blend on low speed of an electric mixer until moistened; increase speed to medium and blend 3 more minutes. Spoon batter into a greased and floured 13"x9" baking pan; set aside. Mix together remaining brown sugar, cinnamon and pecans; sprinkle over batter. Cover and refrigerate overnight.

Bake, uncovered, at 350 degrees for 30 to 40 minutes or until a toothpick inserted in center comes out clean. Makes 12 servings.

Cathy Lemoyne
Ontario, Canada

Sugar Plum Bacon

Make extra of this salty-sweet bacon to serve in sandwiches or crumble over a salad.

½ c. brown sugar, packed
1 t. cinnamon

8 slices bacon, cut in half
   crosswise

Combine brown sugar and cinnamon in a small bowl. Coat each bacon half in sugar mixture. Twist each bacon half and place on a broiler pan lined with aluminum foil.

Bake at 350 degrees for 15 to 20 minutes or until bacon is crisp and sugar is bubbly. Place bacon on a wire rack to cool. Makes 16 pieces.

Karen Pilcher
Burleson, TX

Sausage Gravy

Serve this homestyle gravy over your favorite biscuits for a hearty farmhouse-style breakfast.

1 lb. ground sausage
¼ c. all-purpose flour
3 to 4 c. milk

½ t. salt
¼ t. pepper

Cook sausage in a large skillet over medium-high heat 10 minutes or until browned. Add flour, stirring until mixture thickens.

Reduce heat to medium-low and gradually add milk, stirring constantly, until mixture is thick and bubbly. Add salt and pepper. Serves 4 to 6.

Leslie Stimel
Powell, OH

Homemade Granola

Enjoy granola as a cereal with milk, sprinkled over yogurt or by itself as a snack.

2 c. quick-cooking oats, uncooked
2 c. whole-grain wheat flake cereal
¼ c. wheat germ
1 c. chopped walnuts
1 c. sunflower seeds
1 c. raisins
1 c. flaked coconut
¼ c. butter
1 t. vanilla extract
½ c. honey

Combine first 7 ingredients in a large bowl; pour into an ungreased 13"x9" baking pan.

Add butter, vanilla and honey to a saucepan and cook over low heat until butter and honey are melted; pour over oat mixture. Bake at 350 degrees for 20 minutes, stirring after 10 minutes. Makes about 8½ cups.

Irasema Biggs
Kearney, MO

X's & O's

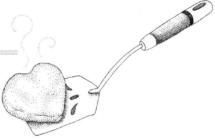

Show little ones you love them…give 'em hugs & kisses! Cut biscuit or sweet roll dough into X's and O's using alphabet cookie cutters. After baking, brush with melted butter and sprinkle with sugar.

Easy Chicken Pot Pie,
page 126

delicious main dishes

It's 5:00 and do you know what's for supper? Of course you do! Over 35 super solutions are at your fingertips…making weeknights a breeze. From the comforts of Easy Chicken Pot Pie (page 126) to crowd-pleasing Southern Pork Barbecue (page 153), these recipes get you in and out of the kitchen…fast!

King Ranch Chicken Casserole

Introduce your family to the cheesy layers of this chicken and tortilla casserole that's popular with residents of the Lone Star State, where it originated.

1 c. onion, diced
1 c. green pepper, diced
8-oz. pkg. sliced mushrooms
¼ c. butter
10¾-oz. can cream of mushroom
   soup
10¾-oz. can cream of chicken
   soup
10-oz. can tomatoes with chiles

1 clove garlic, minced
2 T. chili powder
1 T. chicken broth
12 (6-inch) corn tortillas, torn
   into quarters
3 c. cooked chicken, diced and
   divided
16-oz. pkg. shredded Cheddar
   cheese, divided

Sauté onion, pepper and mushrooms in butter in a large skillet over medium heat. Add soups, tomatoes, garlic, chili powder and broth; heat until bubbly and set aside.

Arrange half the tortilla pieces in a lightly greased 13"x9" baking dish; top with half the chicken, half the sauce and half the cheese. Repeat layers. Bake, uncovered, at 350 degrees for 30 minutes or until hot and bubbly. Serves 6.

Linda Behling
Cecil, PA

well-stocked pantry

Always keep the pantry stocked with canned vegetables, hearty soups, rice and pasta for quick-to-make dishes.

Zesty Roasted Chicken & Potatoes

Just add a salad to round out this quick & easy one-dish meal.

6 boneless, skinless chicken
   breasts
1 lb. redskin potatoes, quartered
⅓ c. mayonnaise
3 T. Dijon mustard

½ t. pepper
2 cloves garlic, pressed
Optional: fresh chives to taste,
   chopped

   Arrange chicken and potatoes in a lightly greased jelly-roll pan. Blend mayonnaise and next 3 ingredients in a small bowl; brush over chicken and potatoes.

   Bake, uncovered, at 400 degrees for 25 to 30 minutes or until potatoes are tender and juices run clear when chicken is pierced with a fork. Sprinkle with chives, if desired. Makes 6 servings.

Denise Mainville
Mesa, AZ

Grilled BBQ Chicken Pizza

The grill is not just for burgers anymore! For a smoky flavor and crispy crust, grilled pizza is the way to go.

13.8-oz. tube refrigerated pizza
   dough
⅔ c. barbecue sauce
2 boneless, skinless chicken
   breasts, cooked and cut into
   strips

8-oz. pkg. shredded mozzarella
   cheese
½ c. green onions, chopped

Spray a baking sheet with no sides with non-stick vegetable spray; roll dough into a 16"x12" rectangle. Spread sauce over dough; arrange cooked chicken strips on top. Sprinkle with shredded cheese.

Spray cold grill with non-stick vegetable spray; preheat grill to medium-low heat (275 to 325 degrees). Place baking sheet on grill; grill, covered, 3 minutes or until dough begins to set (no longer doughy). Slide dough onto grill and continue grilling, covered, 10 more minutes. Use baking sheet to remove pizza from grill; sprinkle with green onions. Slice into squares. Serves 4.

Phyllis Wittig
Quartz Hill, CA

Easy Chicken Pot Pie

(pictured on page 120)

Ready-made pie crusts make this homestyle dish extra easy. A 10-ounce package of frozen oven-roasted diced chicken, thawed, and a 16-ounce package of frozen vegetables can be substituted for the canned chicken and vegetables.

2 (9-inch) refrigerated pie crusts
6¾-oz. can chicken, chopped
16-oz. can mixed vegetables, drained
10¾-oz. can cream of chicken soup

½ t. celery flakes
¼ t. pepper
¼ t. poultry seasoning

Fit one pie crust into a 9" pie plate. Combine chicken and remaining 5 ingredients in a bowl; pour into pie crust.

Moisten edges of bottom crust with water; top with remaining crust. Fold edges under and crimp; cut slits in top. Bake at 400 degrees for 45 to 50 minutes; let stand 10 minutes before serving. Serves 8.

Wanda White
Kings Mountain, NC

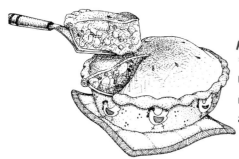

make 'em mini

Use a muffin tin in place of individual casserole dishes when making mini pot pies, quiches or savory popovers. So quick and easy!

Oven Chicken Cordon Bleu

Chopped pecans serve as the breading for this "blue ribbon" favorite.

4 boneless, skinless chicken
   breasts
4 t. Dijon mustard, divided
2 t. garlic, minced and divided

4 slices deli ham
4 slices Swiss cheese
olive oil
1 c. chopped pecans

Place chicken between 2 sheets of heavy-duty plastic wrap; flatten chicken to ¼-inch thickness, using a meat mallet or rolling pin. Top each chicken breast with one teaspoon mustard and ½ teaspoon garlic. Place one ham slice and one cheese slice on each breast; roll up each breast and secure with toothpicks. Brush each roll with oil; roll in pecans. Place in an ungreased 13"x9" baking pan; bake at 350 degrees for 35 to 40 minutes. Serves 4.

Heather Webb
Richmond, VA

Poppy Seed Chicken

This perennial favorite is the go-to recipe for new moms and friends who need a little TLC!

2 lbs. boneless, skinless chicken
   breasts, cooked and cubed
10¾-oz. can cream of chicken
   soup
1 c. sour cream

½ c. butter or margarine, melted
2 T. poppy seed
1 sleeve round buttery crackers,
   crushed and divided

Combine all ingredients in a bowl, reserving ¼ cup cracker crumbs; spread in an ungreased 11"x7" baking pan. Sprinkle with reserved cracker crumbs; bake, uncovered, at 350 degrees for 30 minutes or until thoroughly heated. Serves 6.

Julie Diederich
McPherson, KS

Chicken-Pepper Pasta

Red, yellow and orange bell peppers add color to this creamy pasta dish.

6 T. butter or margarine
1 onion, chopped
1 red pepper, chopped
1 yellow pepper, chopped
1 orange pepper, chopped
1 t. garlic, minced
3 lbs. boneless, skinless chicken
   breasts, cut into strips

1 T. fresh tarragon, minced
¾ t. salt
¼ t. pepper
¾ c. half-and-half
1 c. shredded mozzarella cheese
½ c. grated Parmesan cheese
7-oz. pkg. vermicelli, cooked

"My husband and I love this dish. The aroma is wonderful!"

Pamela

Melt butter in a skillet until sizzling; stir in onion, peppers and garlic. Cook over medium-high heat 2 to 3 minutes or until peppers are crisp-tender. Remove vegetables from skillet with a slotted spoon and set aside.

Add chicken, tarragon, salt and pepper to skillet. Continue cooking, stirring occasionally, 7 to 9 minutes or until chicken is golden and tender. Add vegetables, half-and-half and cheeses to chicken mixture. Reduce heat to medium; continue cooking 3 to 5 minutes or until cheese is melted. Add vermicelli; toss gently to coat. Serve immediately. Serves 4 to 6.

Pamela Chorney
Providence Forge, VA

Italian night

Set a regular theme for each night of the week…Italian Night, Soup & Salad Night, Mexican Night or Casserole Night…based on your family's favorites. It makes meal planning a snap!

Chicken Spaghetti

Broccoli flowerets give this popular recipe color and added nutrients.

1 lb. boneless, skinless chicken breasts, cut into bite-size pieces
¼ to ½ c. butter
1 onion, chopped
8-oz. can sliced mushrooms, drained

16-oz. pkg. broccoli flowerets
1 clove garlic, minced
salt and pepper to taste
16-oz. pkg. spaghetti, cooked
Garnish: grated Parmesan cheese

Sauté chicken in butter in a large skillet over medium-high heat until chicken is no longer pink. Add onion, mushrooms, broccoli and garlic; sauté until chicken is cooked through and vegetables are tender. Add salt and pepper to taste; toss with cooked spaghetti. Sprinkle with Parmesan cheese, if desired. Serves 4.

Glenna Martin
Uwchland, PA

Instant Chicken Parmesan

For Italian Night, spoon over hot spaghetti. Serve with cooked green beans tossed with Italian dressing and sprinkled with grated Parmesan.

28-oz. jar spaghetti sauce
4 to 6 frozen breaded chicken patties

4 to 6 slices provolone cheese
1 to 2 T. grated Parmesan cheese

Spread spaghetti sauce in an ungreased 13"x9" baking pan; arrange frozen chicken patties on top. Place a slice of provolone on top of each patty; sprinkle with Parmesan cheese.

Bake, covered, at 350 degrees for 20 minutes. Uncover and bake 5 to 10 more minutes or until cheese is bubbly. Serves 4 to 6.

Megan Naumovski
Delaware, OH

Creamy Chicken Divan

Chicken divan is simply divine! Spoon each serving over prepared plain rice or long-grain and wild rice.

10-oz. pkg. frozen broccoli
    spears, cooked and drained
1 c. cooked chicken breast, sliced
10¾-oz. can cream of chicken
    soup
¼ t. curry powder

⅓ c. mayonnaise
½ t. lemon juice
¼ c. shredded sharp Cheddar
    cheese
¼ c. soft bread crumbs
1 T. butter, melted

Arrange cooked broccoli in a lightly greased 8"x8" baking pan; place sliced chicken over top. Combine soup, curry powder, mayonnaise and lemon juice; pour over chicken. Sprinkle with cheese.

Combine bread crumbs and butter; sprinkle over top. Bake, uncovered, at 350 degrees for 30 minutes or until heated through. Serves 4.

Lois Bivens
Gooseberry Patch

"I got this recipe years ago at a bridge luncheon from a friend of my mother's. It's easy to double... just use a 13"x9" baking pan."

Lois

favorite recipes

Copy tried & true recipes onto file cards and have them laminated at a copying store. Punch a hole in the upper left corner and thread cards onto a key ring...now you can hang them on the fridge and they'll always be handy.

Chicken & Sausage Étouffée

Chicken and sausage replace crawfish in this version of the popular Cajun dish.

1 T. olive oil
1 onion, chopped
1 green pepper, chopped
2 stalks celery, chopped
1 lb. boneless, skinless chicken
    breasts, cubed
1 lb. smoked sausage, sliced

2 (10-oz.) cans tomatoes with
    chiles
6-oz. can tomato paste
2 (10¾-oz.) cans cream of
    mushroom soup
hot cooked rice

Heat oil in a Dutch oven over medium heat. Add onion, pepper, celery and chicken; cook until juices run clear when chicken is pierced with a fork.

While chicken is cooking, place sausage in a microwave-safe dish with just enough water to cover. Microwave on high 5 minutes; drain sausage and add to chicken mixture.

Add tomatoes to chicken mixture; cook 10 minutes over low heat. Add tomato paste and soup; stir until well blended. Simmer 3 minutes or until bubbly. Serve over hot cooked rice. Makes 4 to 6 servings.

Robin Dusenbery
San Antonio, TX

"This recipe was passed down from my grandmother to my mom to me. Every time I make it, it takes me back to summer days in south Louisiana."

Robin

Lemon & Artichoke Chicken

For preparation ease, look for jars of artichoke hearts in the vegetable aisle of your local supermarket.

2 boneless, skinless chicken
   breasts
3 T. all-purpose flour, divided
2 T. butter
½ c. white wine or chicken broth
2 cloves garlic, minced

⅓ c. lemon juice
½ c. chicken broth
4 artichoke hearts, quartered
4-oz. can sliced mushrooms,
   drained

Place chicken breasts between 2 sheets of heavy-duty plastic wrap; flatten chicken breasts to ¼-inch thickness, using a meat mallet or rolling pin. Lightly coat each chicken breast with one teaspoon flour. Sauté chicken in butter in a skillet over medium-high heat 5 minutes or until golden; remove chicken from skillet.

Stir enough remaining flour into skillet to thicken. Add wine or broth, garlic, lemon juice and chicken broth; stir over low heat until sauce is smooth. Return chicken to skillet; add artichokes and mushrooms. Simmer, covered, 8 to 10 minutes or until juices run clear when chicken is pierced with a fork. Serves 2.

Karen Lee Puchnick
Lyndora, PA

Chicken Club Pasta

Use whatever pasta is in the pantry…rotini, bowtie or penne!

1-lb. pkg. bacon, diced
1½ c. half-and-half
2 to 3 T. dried parsley
¾ c. grated Parmesan cheese
1-lb. pkg. boneless, skinless
   chicken breasts, cooked and
   cubed

Optional: sliced mushrooms
garlic salt and pepper to taste
12- to 16-oz. pkg. pasta, cooked

Fry bacon in a skillet until almost crisp; drain.

Return bacon to skillet; add half-and-half, parsley, cheese, chicken and, if desired, mushrooms. Add garlic salt and pepper to taste.

Reduce heat to low; cook, stirring constantly, 4 minutes. Spoon over cooked pasta; toss to coat. Makes 6 to 8 servings.

Donna Schloemer
Tacoma, WA

Carolyn's Chicken Tetrazzini

An equal amount of turkey, especially leftover holiday turkey, can be substituted for chicken.

2 c. sliced mushrooms	1 t. salt
¼ c. butter	⅛ t. pepper
3 T. all-purpose flour	⅛ t. ground nutmeg
2 c. chicken broth	3 c. cooked chicken, cubed
¼ c. light cream	8-oz. pkg. spaghetti, cooked
3 T. sherry or chicken broth	1 c. grated Parmesan cheese
1 T. fresh parsley, chopped	

Sauté mushrooms in butter in a Dutch oven over medium heat until tender. Stir in flour. Add chicken broth; cook, stirring constantly, until sauce is thickened.

Remove pan from heat; stir in cream, sherry or broth and seasonings. Fold in chicken and cooked spaghetti; turn mixture into a lightly greased 13"x9" baking pan. Sprinkle with Parmesan cheese. Bake, uncovered, at 350 degrees for 30 to 35 minutes or until heated through. Let stand 5 to 10 minutes. Serves 8.

Carolyn Knight
Oklahoma City, OK

Bacon-Wrapped Chicken

Each chicken breast is coated with herb-flavored cream cheese, rolled up and wrapped in bacon, making this dish an excellent choice for special get-togethers.

2 boneless, skinless chicken
   breasts, flattened to ½-inch
   thickness
½ t. salt
¼ t. pepper
2 T. chive-and-onion-flavored
   cream cheese, softened and
   divided

2 T. chilled butter, divided
½ t. dried tarragon, divided
2 slices bacon

Sprinkle chicken with salt and pepper. Spread one tablespoon cream cheese over each chicken breast; top with one tablespoon butter and ¼ teaspoon tarragon. Roll up and wrap with one slice bacon; secure with a toothpick.

Place chicken seam-side down on an ungreased baking sheet; bake at 400 degrees for 30 minutes or until juices run clear when chicken is pierced with a fork. Increase temperature to broil; broil 8 to 10 minutes or until bacon is crisp. Makes 2 servings.

Linda Strausburg
Arroyo Grande, CA

simple sauce

Here's an easy sauce that's just right spooned over Bacon-Wrapped Chicken. Melt a tablespoon of butter and stir in 3 tablespoons Dijon or honey mustard...tangy and oh-so good.

Easy Cheesy Lasagna

No layering of ingredients for this lasagna. You get the same great flavor of a more complicated dish but exert none of the effort.

1 lb. ground beef
26-oz. jar spaghetti sauce
8-oz. pkg. wide egg noodles,
    cooked

8-oz. pkg. shredded mozzarella
    cheese
1 c. cottage cheese
1 c. grated Parmesan cheese

Brown ground beef in a saucepan; drain.

Stir sauce into beef; simmer 5 minutes. Add noodles, mozzarella cheese and cottage cheese; mix well. Place in a greased 2-quart casserole dish. Sprinkle with Parmesan cheese; bake, uncovered, at 350 degrees for 30 minutes. Serves 4 to 6.

Amy Blanchard
Hazel Park, MI

Easy Stromboli

This sandwich includes all your favorite pizza toppings. Serve with warm garlic butter or pizza or spaghetti sauce for dipping.

1 loaf frozen bread dough,
   thawed
2 eggs, separated
2 T. oil
1 t. dried oregano
1 t. dried parsley

½ t. garlic powder
¼ t. pepper
4-oz. pkg. sliced pepperoni
8-oz. pkg. shredded mozzarella
   cheese
1 T. grated Parmesan cheese

Roll bread dough into a 15"x12" rectangle; set aside.

Combine egg yolks, oil, oregano, parsley, garlic powder and pepper; spread over dough. Arrange pepperoni and mozzarella cheese on top; sprinkle with Parmesan cheese.

Roll up dough; place seam-side down on an ungreased baking sheet. Brush with egg whites; bake at 350 degrees for 30 to 40 minutes. Makes 8 servings.

Jane Evans
De Graff, OH

simple tomato sauce

No prepared spaghetti sauce on hand? Try this simple, fresh tomato sauce instead...adjust the veggies to taste and according to how much pasta you're making. Sauté chopped onion and garlic in olive oil until softened. Add chopped tomatoes and simmer 10 minutes. Season with fresh herbs just before serving. So simple!

Beef Stroganoff

With tender meat that's cooked with mushrooms and combined with a sour cream sauce, this main dish will top your family's menu list each week. Spoon over a heap of homestyle egg noodles to serve.

¼ c. all-purpose flour
1 t. paprika
½ t. salt
¼ t. pepper
1-lb. boneless sirloin steak,
    cubed

¼ c. butter
2 cloves garlic, minced
1 c. beef broth
½ c. water
2 c. sliced mushrooms
½ c. sour cream

Combine flour, paprika, salt and pepper in a plastic zipping bag; add sirloin, shaking to coat.

Melt butter in a 12" skillet over medium heat; brown sirloin with garlic. Add broth, water and mushrooms; mix well. Bring to a boil; reduce heat and simmer, covered, 30 minutes or until meat is tender. Uncover and simmer 10 minutes or until thickened. Stir in sour cream; heat thoroughly. Do not boil. Serves 4.

Elizabeth Watters
Edwardsville, IL

Salisbury Steak

Served alongside buttery mashed potatoes...this is a perfect pairing of comfort foods.

1½ lbs. ground beef
¼ c. round buttery crackers, crushed
1 egg, beaten
1 onion, chopped
10¾-oz. can cream of mushroom soup

1 T. prepared mustard
1 T. horseradish sauce
1 t. Worcestershire sauce
½ c. water
2 T. dried parsley

Combine first 4 ingredients; set aside.

Mix together soup, mustard, horseradish sauce and Worcestershire sauce in a medium mixing bowl; add ¼ cup soup mixture to the meat mixture. Form meat into 6 patties.

Brown both sides of patties in a 12" skillet over medium-high heat and drain. Stir water and parsley into the remaining soup mixture; pour over patties. Cook 20 minutes or until heated through. Makes 6 servings.

Missy Alleman
Lewisville, OH

Baked Ziti Supreme

Keep these ingredients on hand for a quick weeknight meal. While the ziti is cooking, the ground beef mixture can be browning; then stir together, and it's ready to bake.

1 lb. ground beef
1 onion, chopped
28-oz. jar spaghetti sauce with mushrooms

1½ c. shredded mozzarella cheese, divided
5 c. cooked ziti
¼ c. grated Parmesan cheese

Cook beef and onion in a skillet over medium heat until beef is browned; drain and return to skillet.

Stir spaghetti sauce, one cup mozzarella cheese and cooked ziti into skillet; mix well. Spoon into a lightly greased 3-quart casserole dish; sprinkle with remaining mozzarella cheese and Parmesan cheese. Bake, uncovered, at 350 degrees for 25 to 30 minutes. Serves 6.

Jessica Parker
Mulvane, KS

Saucy Meatloaf

The tangy steak sauce is what gives this meatloaf its terrific flavor.

1½ lbs. ground beef
1 egg, beaten
1 c. soft bread crumbs
½ c. milk
3 T. red steak sauce

1¼ t. salt
⅛ t. pepper
2 T. red steak sauce
Garnish: additional red steak
    sauce

Combine first 8 ingredients; place in a lightly greased 9"x5" loaf pan. Bake at 350 degrees for one hour, brushing top with additional steak sauce, if desired. Let meatloaf stand 5 minutes before slicing. Serves 6 to 8.

Gloria Schantz
Breinigsville, PA

meatloaf sandwiches

Cut meatloaf into thick slices, wrap individually and freeze. Later, they can be thawed and rewarmed quickly for scrumptious meatloaf sandwiches at a few moments' notice.

Country-Fried Steak

The key to cooking these crispy steaks is to not crowd them in the skillet.

1½ c. all-purpose flour
1 t. paprika
1 T. salt
¼ t. pepper
2 lbs. beef cube steak, cut into
    8 pieces

1 c. milk
¼ c. oil
2.6-oz. pkg. country-style gravy
    mix, prepared

Combine flour, paprika, salt and pepper; set aside. Dip steak into milk, then into flour mixture, pressing to coat completely.

Heat oil in a large skillet over medium heat; add steak, in batches, and cook 5 minutes on each side or until golden and tender, adding additional oil as needed. Top with prepared gravy. Makes 8 servings.

Dana Thompson
Gooseberry Patch

"Don't forget all the things that go with this...mashed potatoes, corn on the cob and rolls with butter."

Dana

family mealtime

Over dinner, ask your children to tell you about books they're reading at school and return the favor by sharing books you loved as a child. You may find you have some favorites in common!

Citrus-Grilled Pork Tenderloin

A savory-sweet flavor is what sets this grilled tenderloin apart from the rest. The savory comes from the garlic and soy sauce and the sweet from the orange marmalade and a hint of fresh mint.

1-lb. pork tenderloin, cut into ¾-inch-thick slices
½ t. pepper
⅔ c. orange marmalade

¼ c. fresh mint, chopped
¼ c. soy sauce
4 cloves garlic, minced

Sprinkle pork slices with pepper. Combine marmalade and remaining 3 ingredients; stir well. Brush over pork, reserving remaining marmalade mixture.

Spray cold grill with non-stick vegetable spray; preheat grill to medium-high heat (350 to 400 degrees). Grill pork, covered, 3 minutes per side or until no longer pink. Baste frequently with reserved marmalade mixture.

Place remaining marmalade mixture in a saucepan and bring to a boil over medium heat; cook one minute. Drizzle over pork. Serves 4.

Jo Ann
Gooseberry Patch

handy kitchen tools

Keep kitchen scissors nearby...they make short work of snipping fresh herbs, chopping green onions or even cutting up whole tomatoes right in the can.

Sweet & Tangy Pork

Serve over cooked rice and add a side of steamed sugar snap peas for a complete meal.

1 T. oil
4 boneless pork steaks
10¾-oz. can tomato soup
2 T. vinegar
1 T. Worcestershire sauce

1 T. brown sugar
8-oz. can pineapple tidbits, drained and ¼ c. juice reserved

Heat oil in a skillet over medium heat. Add steaks and cook until golden on both sides; drain.

Stir soup, vinegar, Worcestershire sauce, brown sugar, pineapple and reserved juice into skillet. Cover and simmer over low heat 5 to 10 minutes or until pork is cooked through. Makes 4 servings.

Cheryl Brady
Canfield, OH

dinner art

Looking for something to keep the kids busy while you're making dinner? Just toss out a roll of kraft paper and plenty of crayons...they can create a tablecloth masterpiece!

Easy Spaghetti & Meatballs

One taste of this homemade sauce, and family & friends will think that it has simmered all day long. You don't have to share that it only took 20 minutes!

10-oz. pkg. spaghetti, uncooked
24 frozen, cooked Italian-style
    meatballs, thawed
2 (14-oz.) cans Italian-style diced
    tomatoes, undrained
2 (6-oz.) cans tomato paste

½ c. water
2 t. dried Italian seasoning
2 t. sugar
Optional: shredded Parmesan
    cheese

Cook pasta according to package directions; keep warm.

Meanwhile, add meatballs and next 5 ingredients to a Dutch oven. Cook over medium heat 20 minutes, stirring occasionally. Serve over hot cooked pasta. Sprinkle with Parmesan cheese, if desired. Serves 4 to 6.

Stephanie Whisenhunt
Birmingham, AL

Pork & Apple Skillet Supper

Add a side of shredded cabbage that's been sautéed in butter for a satisfying combination with pork & apples.

2 T. butter
½ t. garlic, minced
½ t. salt
¼ t. pepper

4 (3- to 4-oz.) pork cube steaks
1 onion, sliced
2 Granny Smith apples, cored
 and sliced

Melt butter in a skillet until sizzling; stir in garlic, salt and pepper. Add pork steaks and onion. Cook over medium-high heat 4 to 6 minutes or until pork is browned, turning occasionally.

Add apples to skillet; continue cooking 2 to 3 minutes or just until tender, stirring occasionally. Place pork steaks on plates; top with apples and onion. Serves 4.

Carol Lytle
Columbus, OH

Pork Schnitzel

Schnitzel is the German term for "cutlet." It describes a thin slice of meat that's dipped in an egg mixture, breaded and fried. Irene suggests serving with fresh green beans, applesauce and hot, buttery rolls...yum!

6 (½-inch-thick) boneless
    pork chops
½ t. salt
⅓ c. all-purpose flour

¼ c. dry bread crumbs
1 egg
¼ c. milk
3 T. oil

Place pork chops between 2 sheets of heavy-duty plastic wrap; flatten to ⅛-inch thickness, using a meat mallet or rolling pin; season both sides with salt.

Combine flour and bread crumbs; set aside. Whisk egg and milk together in a pie plate; set aside. Dip pork chops into egg mixture; coat with crumb mixture. Brown both sides of pork chops in oil in a 12" skillet over medium-high heat about 3 minutes per side. Remove to a serving platter; serve immediately. Makes 6 servings.

Irene Robinson
Cincinnati, OH

help yourself

Food for friends doesn't have to be fancy. Your guests will be delighted with comfort foods like Grandma used to make. Invite them to help themselves from large platters, skillets and casserole dishes set right on the table...so family-friendly!

Southern Pork Barbecue

Good-tasting barbecue isn't always smoked on a grill...the slow cooker does the job just fine!

3-lb. boneless pork loin roast, trimmed
1 c. water
18-oz. bottle barbecue sauce
2 T. Worcestershire sauce
1 to 2 T. hot pepper sauce

¼ c. brown sugar, packed
½ t. salt
1 t. pepper
8 to 10 hamburger buns, split
Optional: deli coleslaw

Place roast in a 3½- to 4-quart slow cooker; add one cup water. Cover and cook on high setting 7 hours or until tender.

Shred meat; return to slow cooker. Stir in sauces, sugar, salt and pepper; cover and cook on low setting one more hour. Serve on buns and top with coleslaw, if desired. Makes 8 to 10 servings.

Vicki Chavis
Fort Myers, FL

"My whole family loves this recipe and my friends ask for it by name. It's a great way to serve a few people or many."

Vicki

Scalloped Potatoes & Ham

Serve this favorite duo as a one-dish meal or as a hearty side dish.

8 potatoes, peeled and sliced
2 c. cooked ham, cubed
2 c. onion, diced
2 c. shredded Cheddar cheese

2 (10¾-oz.) cans cream of
    mushroom soup
¼ t. salt
¼ t. pepper

Stir together all ingredients and place in a 5-quart slow cooker. Cover and cook on low setting 6 hours. Serves 6 to 8.

Pam Colden
Brodhead, WI

welcome basket

Invite new neighbors to share your next slow-cooker meal. Send them home with a gift basket filled with flyers from favorite bakeries and pizza parlors, coupons and local maps…tuck in a package of homemade cookies. So thoughtful!

Pepper-Crusted Salmon

You'll want to use freshly ground pepper for a crispy crust.

¼ c. soy sauce
2 cloves garlic, pressed
4 t. lemon juice
2 t. sugar

4 (6-oz.) salmon fillets
1 T. freshly ground pepper
¼ c. olive oil

Combine first 4 ingredients in a plastic zipping bag; add salmon. Refrigerate 10 minutes. Remove salmon from bag; discard marinade. Pat salmon dry. Press pepper into both sides of salmon.

Heat oil in a large heavy skillet over medium heat; sauté salmon 2 to 3 minutes per side or until it flakes easily with a fork. Drain on paper towels. Serves 4.

Stacie Avner
Delaware, OH

Baked Salmon Patties

This old-fashioned quick & easy recipe calls for baking the patties instead of frying them. The result is the same golden patties...every bit as tasty as you remember them.

14¾-oz. can salmon, drained and
   flaked
1 c. soft bread crumbs
½ c. green onions, diced

1 egg, beaten
2 T. lemon juice
1 t. Worcestershire sauce

Mix together all ingredients; shape into 4 patties.

Place patties on a greased baking sheet; bake at 400 degrees for 5 to 6 minutes. Turn and bake 5 to 6 more minutes or until golden and heated through. Makes 4.

Lisa Bownas
Dublin, OH

Fried Catfish

Invite friends over for an old-fashioned fish fry! Kick up the flavor by adding the Cajun seasoning. Don't forget to include Hushpuppies.

3 lbs. catfish fillets	1 T. salt
12-oz. can beer	1 T. pepper
2 T. baking soda	Optional: 2 T. Cajun seasoning
2 c. milk	8-oz. pkg. fish breading mix
1 egg	oil for frying

Soak fish in beer and baking soda one hour.

Combine milk, egg, salt, pepper and, if desired, Cajun seasoning. Drain fish and dip into milk mixture, then dredge in breading mix.

Pour oil to a depth of 2 inches in a large skillet. Heat oil to 375 degrees; fry fish, a few fillets at a time, until golden. Serves 5.

Debbie Nemecek
Springfield, IL

"My dad fishes all summer and brings home freezer bags full of fish fillets. Everyone loves it prepared this way and they beg for more!"

Debbie

Hushpuppies

Legend has it that these fritters got their name from fishermen sitting around the campfire frying fish. They shushed their dogs by throwing scraps of fried cornmeal batter to them and saying, "Hush, puppies!"

2 c. yellow cornmeal	1 egg
1 c. all-purpose flour	14¾-oz. can cream-style corn
¼ c. sugar	salt and pepper to taste
1 T. baking powder	oil for deep frying
1 T. onion, minced	

Mix all ingredients except oil in a large bowl. Pour oil to a depth of 2 inches in a large skillet. Heat oil to 375 degrees. Drop batter by tablespoonfuls into hot oil; fry until golden. Makes about 3 dozen.

Sandy Fine
Columbia, MO

"These hushpuppies are really good at a fish fry, especially with catfish! They're a real crowd pleaser."

Sandy

Janet Sue's Crab Cakes

Lump crabmeat, whole pieces of white crabmeat, is the preferred choice for crab cakes. Serve these cakes with a squeeze of lemon or your favorite sauce to enhance the cakes' delicate flavor.

3 lbs. fresh crabmeat	2 T. dry mustard
1¼ c. mayonnaise	¾ c. pimentos, diced
3 eggs	1 c. green pepper, diced
¼ c. onion, minced	1 T. Worcestershire sauce
¾ t. seasoned salt	1¼ c. dry bread crumbs
⅛ t. pepper	Optional: lemon wedges

Separate and flake the crabmeat with a fork; set aside.

Combine mayonnaise and next 8 ingredients in a bowl. Add crabmeat; mix well. Fold in bread crumbs; divide into 16 portions and shape into patties.

Arrange on an ungreased baking sheet and bake at 425 degrees for 10 to 15 minutes or until golden. Serve with lemon wedges, if desired. Makes 16.

Janet Sue Burns
Granbury, TX

quick side

A crisp green salad goes well with all kinds of comforting main dishes. For a zippy lemon dressing, shake up ½ cup olive oil, ⅓ cup fresh lemon juice and a tablespoon of Dijon mustard in a small jar and chill to blend.

Shrimp & Mushroom Fettuccine

Portabella mushrooms add meaty flavor and texture to dishes. Be sure to remove the gills (the portion underneath the mushroom's cap) before slicing and adding the mushroom to the sauce...the gills will darken a light-colored sauce.

1 T. olive oil
1 portabella mushroom, sliced
1 c. onion, finely chopped
¼ c. fresh Italian parsley, chopped
¼ t. salt
1 clove garlic, minced

1 c. chicken broth
¼ c. sherry or chicken broth
1 lb. uncooked large shrimp, peeled and cleaned
8-oz. pkg. fettuccine, cooked
½ c. grated Parmesan cheese
1 T. fresh chives, chopped

Heat oil in a large saucepan over medium-high heat. Add mushroom, onion, parsley, salt and garlic; sauté 4 minutes or until onion is tender, stirring frequently.

Stir in broth, sherry or broth and shrimp; bring to a boil. Add fettuccine; cook 3 minutes or until shrimp turn pink, tossing to combine. Sprinkle with cheese and chives. Serves 4.

Diana Chaney
Olathe, KS

"I like to keep frozen packages of peeled, uncooked shrimp on hand for quick, delicious meals...just thaw according to package directions."

Diana

Louisiana Shrimp

Serve lots of French bread with these shrimp to soak up the saucy seasonings.

2 T. butter
½ c. Worcestershire sauce
5 cloves garlic, chopped
6 bay leaves, broken in half
2 t. seafood seasoning

hot pepper sauce to taste
pepper to taste
2 T. lemon juice
1 lb. uncooked shrimp, peeled
    and cleaned

Combine all ingredients except shrimp in a saucepan; mix well. Bring to a boil; reduce heat and simmer 5 minutes.

Place shrimp in an ungreased 13"x9" casserole dish; pour mixture over shrimp. Bake at 400 degrees for 10 minutes. Remove and discard bay leaves. Serves 2.

Deborah DeVaughn
Martin, TN

Texas 2-Step Apple Crisp,
page 197

slow cookin'... fast!

A slow cooker simmering away means that at the end of the day, a hearty, homestyle meal awaits you and your family with practically no effort at all. What a time saver! Rediscover family favorites like Slow-Cooker Chicken Chili (page 172) and French Dip au Jus (page 183)...and make surprising new discoveries in your slow cooker like Fudgy Pudding Cake (page 195) and Unbelievable Caramel Pie (page 199). Fall back in love with this time-tested way of cooking, and enjoy dinner the quick & easy way!

Easy Slow-Cooker Bean Dip

This will be a favorite at potlucks and family gatherings. It's a good thing this dip makes a lot, because family & friends won't be able to get enough of its creamy, cheesy flavor.

4 (16-oz.) cans refried beans
2 (8-oz.) pkgs. Colby Jack cheese
  cubes
1¼-oz. pkg. taco seasoning mix

1 bunch green onions, chopped
1 c. sour cream
8-oz. pkg. cream cheese, cubed

Place all ingredients in a 3½-quart slow cooker; stir to mix. Cover and cook on low setting 2½ hours. Stir often. Makes 11 cups.

Marni Senner
Long Beach, CA

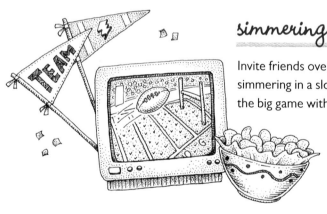

simmering good eats

Invite friends over for snacks on game day. With hearty appetizers simmering in a slow cooker or 2, you'll be able to relax and enjoy the big game with your guests!

Berry Good Wild Rice

Mushrooms, almonds and dried cranberries add extra flavor to the wild rice. It's a good choice for a holiday dinner.

1½ c. wild rice, uncooked
2 (14-oz.) cans vegetable broth
4½-oz. can sliced mushrooms, drained
4 green onions, sliced

1 T. butter, melted
½ t. salt
¼ t. pepper
½ c. slivered almonds
⅓ c. sweetened dried cranberries

Mix first 7 ingredients in a 3-quart slow cooker. Cover and cook on low setting 5 hours or until rice is tender. Stir in almonds and cranberries. Cover and cook on low setting 15 more minutes. If all liquid is not absorbed, serve rice with a slotted spoon. Makes 7 cups.

Judith Jennings
Ironwood, MI

"Try it...you'll never go back to plain old white rice!"

Judith

Stewed Black-Eyed Peas

Dried black-eyed peas and beans are good options for slow cooking, as they soak up flavors from other ingredients during the long simmering time.

1 lb. dried black-eyed peas
1 lb. andouille sausage, cut into ¼-inch slices
1 c. yellow onion, chopped
½ t. salt
2 T. hot pepper sauce

5 cloves garlic, pressed
4 bay leaves
1 t. dried thyme
1 t. dried parsley
8 c. chicken broth

Sort and wash peas. Cover with water 2 inches above peas; let soak 8 hours. Drain and place peas in a 5-quart slow cooker.

Add sausage and remaining ingredients to peas in slow cooker. Cover and cook on high setting 4 hours. Discard bay leaves. Makes 8 cups.

Leslie Stimel
Powell, OH

Savory Southern-Style Greens

Be sure to save the cooking broth…it's a flavorful substitute for water when cooking rice.

2 smoked ham hocks
6 c. water, divided
3 cubes ham bouillon
2 T. sugar
2 T. vinegar brine from a jar of
    sliced jalapeño peppers

½ t. pepper
1 bunch collard greens, trimmed
    and sliced into ½-inch strips
Optional: cooked rice

"For best flavor, cool and refrigerate greens overnight; reheat the next day at serving time."

Staci

Combine ham hocks and 6 cups water in a stockpot; bring to a boil. Reduce heat and simmer 15 to 30 minutes. Stir in ham bouillon cubes, sugar, brine and pepper.

Transfer ham hocks and greens to a 5-quart slow cooker; pour cooking liquid over top. Cover and cook on low setting 8 hours or until greens are tender but not mushy, adding more water as necessary to keep crock at least half full of liquid. Remove ham hocks; dice meat and return to slow cooker. Serve over cooked rice, if desired. Makes 9 cups.

Staci Meyers
Cocoa, FL

Mexicali Rice

This rice is packed with colorful ingredients and bold flavors...it's a good complement to simple entrées. Converted rice works best here and in most slow-cooker recipes because it holds its shape better.

1 c. onion, chopped
1 c. red pepper, chopped
2 c. converted long-grain rice, uncooked
15¼-oz. can corn, drained
15-oz. can black beans, drained and rinsed
4.5-oz. can diced green chiles, drained

3½ c. boiling water
½ c. frozen orange juice concentrate
¼ c. lime juice
1 T. chili powder
1 t. salt
1½ t. ground cumin
⅓ c. fresh cilantro, chopped
lime wedges

Place onion in a medium microwave-safe bowl; cover loosely with heavy-duty plastic wrap. Microwave on high 2 minutes or until tender.

Combine onion, red pepper and next 10 ingredients in a 3½- to 4-quart slow cooker. Cover and cook on low setting 2½ to 3 hours or until rice is tender and liquid is absorbed. Add cilantro; fluff with a fork until blended. Serve with lime wedges. Serves 10 to 12.

Marian Buckley
Fontana, CA

tried & true gift

A slow cooker makes a super gift! Before wrapping it up, be sure to tuck in some favorite tried & true recipes...they'll be so appreciated.

Zesty Macaroni & Cheese

Reheat any leftovers in the microwave, adding milk as needed to maintain its creamy texture.

1 c. onion, minced
16-oz. pkg. elbow macaroni, cooked
16-oz. pkg. pasteurized process cheese spread, cubed
8-oz. pkg. Pepper Jack cheese, cubed
2 (10¾-oz.) cans Cheddar cheese soup

Place onion in a microwave-safe bowl; cover loosely with heavy-duty plastic wrap. Microwave on high 2½ minutes or until tender.

Combine cooked macaroni, cheese spread and Pepper Jack cheese in a 4- to 5-quart slow cooker. Stir in soup; add onion. Cover and cook on high setting 2 hours. Stir occasionally. Serves 10 to 12.

Jen Licon-Connor
Gooseberry Patch

"If you want to make this recipe extra zesty, add ½ cup salsa or stir in green chiles to taste!"

Jen

Country Cornbread Dressing

To save time, purchase cornbread from your supermarket deli...just be sure that it's savory, not sweet, cornbread.

6½ c. cornbread, crumbled
8 slices day-old bread, torn
4 eggs, beaten
1 onion, chopped
1 stalk celery, chopped
2½ c. chicken broth
2 (10¾-oz.) cans cream of chicken soup
1 T. dried sage
1 t. salt
¼ t. pepper
2 T. butter or margarine, sliced

Combine all ingredients except butter in a very large bowl; mix well. Spoon into a 5- to 6-quart slow cooker; dot with butter. Cover and cook on low setting 6 hours. Serves 8 to 10.

Tracy Chitwood
Van Buren, MO

"The best dressing I've ever tasted...and so easy, too!"

Tracy

Collins' Best Lentil Soup

Thanks to the hearty ingredients this soup offers, appetites are sure to be satisfied.

1 c. dried lentils
14-oz. pkg. turkey Kielbasa,
　 sliced ½-inch thick
1 c. onion, chopped
1 c. celery, chopped
1 c. carrots, peeled and chopped

1 c. redskin potato, diced
2 T. fresh flat-leaf parsley,
　 chopped
6 c. beef broth
½ t. pepper
⅛ t. ground nutmeg

Sort and wash lentils. Combine lentils, sausage and remaining ingredients in a 3-quart slow cooker. Cover and cook on high setting one hour; reduce heat to low setting and cook 3 hours. Stir before serving. Makes 10½ cups.

Michelle Collins
San Diego, CA

"This recipe reminds me of a very good friend of mine...he used to make a lentil & sausage soup that I adored."

Michelle

3-Meat Slow-Cooker Chili

Ground beef, sausage and bacon make up the base of this robust chili. Spoon it over a bed of rice or handful of taco chips...it feeds a crowd!

1 lb. ground beef, browned
1 lb. ground sausage, browned
1 lb. bacon, crisply cooked and
    crumbled
4 (15-oz.) cans tomato sauce

3 (16-oz.) cans kidney beans,
    drained and rinsed
2 T. chili seasoning
15¼-oz. can corn, drained

Place first 3 ingredients in a greased 6-quart slow cooker; stir in tomato sauce and next 2 ingredients. Cover and cook on low setting 4 to 6 hours; add corn during last hour. Makes 13½ cups.

Beth Goblirsch
Minneapolis, MN

Slow-Cooker Chicken Chili

For a thicker chili, mash and stir the beans before serving. Add creaminess by stirring in sour cream and Monterey Jack cheese.

1 c. dried Great Northern beans
1 lb. boneless, skinless chicken
    breasts, cubed
1 clove garlic, minced
1 onion, chopped
2 t. dried oregano
½ t. salt

10¾-oz. can cream of chicken
    soup
5 c. water or chicken broth
1 t. ground cumin
4.5-oz. can diced green chiles
2 t. hot pepper sauce

Sort and wash beans. Combine beans, chicken and next 8 ingredients in a 5-quart slow cooker. Cover and cook on high setting one hour; reduce heat to low setting and cook 6 hours. Stir in hot sauce. Makes 9 cups.

Erin Williams
Bayview, WI

Hearty Beef Stew

Abundant in vegetables and flavor, this one-dish stew is all you need for a satisfying meal.

3 carrots, peeled and sliced
3 potatoes, diced
1 onion, chopped
2 stalks celery, sliced
2 lbs. stew beef, cubed
¼ c. all-purpose flour
1½ t. salt
½ t. pepper

1 clove garlic, minced
1 bay leaf
1 c. beef broth
1 t. paprika
1 t. Worcestershire sauce
2 t. browning and seasoning
   sauce

"Filled with vegetables, this recipe is a good way to get the kids to eat their veggies!"

Connie

Arrange vegetables in a 5- to 6-quart slow cooker; top with beef. Combine flour, salt and pepper; sprinkle over meat and stir well. Add garlic and remaining ingredients. Cover and cook on high setting one hour; reduce heat to low setting and cook 6 hours. Remove and discard bay leaf. Makes 9 cups.

Connie Knepp
Yeagertown, PA

suitable sizes

Slow cookers come in so many sizes…round and oval, and from 16 ounces to 7 quarts with half sizes in between…you might want to have more than one! A 3-quart size is handy for sauces and recipes that will feed about 4 people, while a 5- to 6-quart one is terrific for larger yields.

Jammin' Jambalaya

Jambalaya is touted by many as the trademark dish of Cajun cooking. As with gumbo, you're likely to come across many combinations of ingredients for this seasoned rice dish...this version uses chicken, andouille sausage and shrimp.

1 lb. boneless, skinless chicken
    breasts, cubed
1 lb. andouille sausage, sliced
28-oz. can diced tomatoes
1 onion, chopped
1 green pepper, chopped
1 c. celery, chopped
1 c. chicken broth

2 t. Cajun seasoning
2 t. dried oregano
2 t. dried parsley
1 t. cayenne pepper
½ t. dried thyme
1 lb. frozen cooked shrimp,
    thawed and tails removed
cooked rice

"Yum! This feeds a crowd...and everybody loves it!"

Valarie

Place chicken and next 6 ingredients in a 5-quart slow cooker. Stir in seasonings; mix well. Cover and cook on high setting one hour; reduce heat to low setting and cook 6 hours. Add shrimp during final 30 minutes of cooking. Serve over cooked rice. Makes 11 cups.

Valarie Dennard
Palatka, FL

Lemony "Baked" Chicken

A perfectly golden chicken is the result of slow cooking this main dish. Stir a little lemon zest and chopped parsley into steamed rice for a perfect side dish.

3½- to 4-lb. roasting chicken
2 T. olive oil
1 lemon, halved
2 cloves garlic, minced
1 t. dried parsley

1 t. salt
½ t. pepper
Garnishes: additional lemon
    halves and parsley

Pat chicken dry with a paper towel; rub with oil. Place lemon halves inside chicken cavity; tie ends of legs together with a string and tuck wing tips under. Place chicken in a 5-quart oval slow cooker. Sprinkle with seasonings. Cover and cook on high setting one hour; reduce heat to low setting and cook 4½ hours or until a thermometer inserted into thigh registers 180 degrees. Garnish, if desired. Serves 4.

Sharon Lundberg
Longwood, FL

slow-cooker safety

When cooking raw meat and poultry, the USDA recommends using high heat for the first hour of cooking to ensure ingredients reach a safe temperature quickly. Then reduce the heat to low for the remainder of the cooking time. Omit starting on high heat for the first hour if meat is browned first…precooking jump-starts the initial temperature of the ingredients.

Coq au Vin

This slow-cooker version of the classic French dish is filled with rich flavor.

4 boneless, skinless chicken
    breasts
16-oz. pkg. sliced mushrooms
15-oz. jar pearl onions, drained
½ c. dry white wine or chicken
    broth
1 t. dried thyme

½ t. salt
½ t. pepper
1 bay leaf
1 c. chicken broth
⅓ c. all-purpose flour
cooked rice
Optional: fresh parsley, chopped

"Elegant enough for guests."
Kendall

Place chicken in a 5-quart oval slow cooker; top with mushrooms and onions. Drizzle with wine or broth and sprinkle with thyme, salt and pepper; add bay leaf. Stir together broth and flour; pour into slow cooker. Cover and cook on high setting one hour; reduce heat to low setting and cook 3 hours. Discard bay leaf. Serve over rice; sprinkle with parsley, if desired. Serves 4.

Kendall Hale
Lynn, MA

Sweet-and-Sour Pork

(pictured on opposite page)

No need for take-out when this popular Asian dish is ready and waiting in the slow cooker.

1 onion, chopped
1½ lbs. pork loin, cubed
14-oz. can chicken broth
10-oz. bottle sweet-and-sour
  sauce

15¼-oz. can pineapple chunks,
  drained
2 green peppers, chopped
1 c. converted rice, uncooked

Place onion in a 5-quart slow cooker; top with pork, broth and sauce. Cover and cook on high setting one hour; reduce heat to low setting and cook 3½ hours. Add pineapple, green peppers and rice; mix well. Cover and cook on low setting 1½ more hours. . Serves 4 to 6.

Janice Dorsey
San Antonio, TX

Finger-Lickin' Ribs

Standing ribs along the sides of the cooker gives them direct contact with heat, resulting in crispy brown edges...similar to smoked ribs.

3 to 4 lbs. baby back pork ribs,
  racks cut in half
8-oz. bottle Russian dressing
¾ c. pineapple juice

1 t. salt
1 t. pepper
½ t. garlic salt

"Slice into individual ribs to serve as appetizers...yum!"

Brad

Place one rack of ribs in bottom of a 6-quart slow cooker; stand remaining rib racks on their sides around edges of slow cooker.

Stir together dressing and remaining ingredients; pour over ribs. Cover and cook on high setting one hour; reduce heat to low setting and cook 5 hours. Skim fat from drippings. Serve ribs with sauce. Serves 8 to 10.

Brad Daugherty
Columbus, OH

Holiday Cranberry Pork Roast

Cranberry sauce and juice impart a sweet flavor to this savory pork roast…it's a delicious change from roast turkey during the holidays.

2½-lb. boneless pork loin roast
16-oz. can jellied cranberry sauce
½ c. cranberry juice cocktail
½ c. sugar
1 t. dry mustard

¼ t. ground cloves
2 T. cornstarch
2 T. cold water
1 t. salt

Place pork in a 5-quart oval slow cooker. Stir together cranberry sauce and next 4 ingredients. Pour cranberry mixture over pork. Cover and cook on high setting one hour; reduce heat to low setting and cook 4½ hours or until pork is tender.

Skim fat from drippings in slow cooker. Measure drippings to equal 2 cups, adding water if necessary. Pour drippings into a medium saucepan; bring to a boil over medium-high heat. Stir together cornstarch and cold water until smooth; add to drippings and cook over medium-high heat, stirring constantly, 2 to 3 minutes or until thickened. Stir in salt. Serve gravy with sliced pork. Serves 4 to 6.

Patricia Wissler
Harrisburg, PA

no peeking!

Don't remove the slow-cooker lid unless you're stirring or checking for doneness. Every time the cover comes off, you lose heat that's equal to 20 to 30 minutes of cooking time…so trust the recipe.

Pork Marengo

Marengo has French origins and usually indicates a dish that's sautéed in olive oil and then braised with tomatoes, olives and garlic. This recipe is similar, braising pork in a slow cooker. History has it that Napoleon's chef created the original dish after the Battle of Marengo in 1800.

2 lbs. boneless pork shoulder, cubed
1 yellow onion, chopped
2 T. oil
14½-oz. can diced tomatoes
1 c. sliced mushrooms
1 t. chicken bouillon granules
1 t. dried marjoram

½ t. dried thyme
⅛ t. pepper
⅓ c. cold water
3 T. all-purpose flour
¾ t. salt
½ t. pepper
cooked rice or pasta

Cook pork cubes and onion in oil in a skillet over medium heat until browned. Drain and place pork mixture in a 3½- to 4-quart slow cooker; set aside.

Place tomatoes and next 5 ingredients in skillet; cook, stirring to scrape up bits from bottom of skillet. Pour over pork in slow cooker. Cover and cook on low setting 8 hours.

Stir together water and flour; stir into pork. Add salt and pepper. Increase heat to high setting and cook, uncovered, 15 to 20 minutes or until thickened, stirring occasionally. Serve over cooked rice or pasta. Makes 4 servings.

Penny Sherman
Cumming, GA

French Dip au Jus

The roast in these sandwiches is melt-in-your-mouth tender, and the brown sugar added to the broth pumps up the flavor! For party-size sandwiches, substitute smaller rolls.

3½- to 4-lb. sirloin tip roast
2 c. beef broth
⅔ c. brown sugar, packed
¼ t. seasoning salt

1 t. liquid smoke
⅓ c. soy sauce
12 hoagie buns, split
12 slices Swiss cheese

Place roast in a 5-quart slow cooker. Stir together broth and next 4 ingredients and pour over roast. Cover and cook on high setting one hour; reduce heat to low setting and cook 9 hours.

Remove roast from slow cooker, reserving broth; shred roast with 2 forks. Place shredded meat evenly on hoagie buns and top with Swiss cheese. Serve with reserved broth for dipping. Serves 12.

Terri Vanden Bosch
Rock Valley, IA

what's for dinner?

Tossing tonight's dinner into a slow cooker is a guaranteed way to have a family-style dinner with minimum fuss and preparation throughout the day.

Jackie's Apple Corned Beef

Potatoes, carrots and onion add heartiness and savory flavor to this traditional Irish-American dish.

8 new redskin potatoes
4 to 5 carrots, peeled and cut into chunks
1 onion, cut into 8 wedges
3-lb. corned beef brisket

4 c. apple juice
1 c. brown sugar, packed
1 T. Dijon or honey mustard
Sautéed Cabbage

Arrange potatoes, carrots and onion wedges in a 5-quart slow cooker; top with corned beef. Stir together apple juice, brown sugar and mustard; pour over top. Cover and cook on high setting one hour; reduce heat to low setting and cook 8 hours.

Slice meat thinly across the grain. Serve with cooked vegetables, Sautéed Cabbage and broth. Makes 4 to 6 servings.

Sautéed Cabbage:

½ head cabbage, shredded
½ c. onion, chopped
1 to 2 cloves garlic, minced

2 T. butter
1 t. salt
½ t. pepper

Sauté cabbage, onion and garlic in butter in a skillet over medium-high heat until soft. Add salt and pepper; serve warm.

Mary Lauff-Thompson
Philadelphia, PA

Slow-Cooker Enchiladas

This cheesy casserole is layered with familiar south-of-the-border ingredients. For added crunch, serve with tortilla chips.

1 lb. ground chuck
½ c. onion, chopped
10-oz. can enchilada sauce
10¾-oz. can nacho cheese soup
10¾-oz. can cream of mushroom
  soup
15¼-oz. can corn, drained

16-oz. can pinto beans, drained
  and rinsed
½ c. sliced black olives
8 (5½-inch) corn tortillas
2 c. shredded Cheddar cheese,
  divided

Cook ground chuck and onion until beef is done and onion is tender; drain and set aside.

Combine beef mixture and next 6 ingredients. Place one tortilla in the bottom of a 3- to 4-quart round slow cooker; spoon one-eighth of the beef mixture over tortilla, followed by ¼ cup of cheese. Repeat layers until all ingredients are used, ending with cheese. Cover and cook on high setting one hour until cheese is melted and bubbling. Serves 6 to 8.

Laura Harp
Bolivar, MO

slow-cooking tip

Remember that one hour on the high setting is equivalent to 2 hours on the low setting. So adjust recipes according to your time frame. A bonus to cooking on the low setting is that recipes can generally cook a bit longer than the recipe states without becoming overdone.

Fiesta Beef Fajitas

Flavorful skirt steak is traditional in fajitas, but if your grocery doesn't carry it, flank steak is also a good choice.

2 lbs. beef skirt
14½-oz. can tomatoes with chiles
2 (1.12-oz.) pkgs. fajita seasoning
   mix
1 onion, vertically sliced
2 green peppers, sliced into strips

8 to 12 (10-inch) flour tortillas,
   warmed
Garnishes: guacamole, sour
   cream, shredded cheese,
   salsa, shredded lettuce

Place beef in a 4-quart slow cooker and set aside.

Stir together tomatoes and fajita seasoning mix in a bowl; pour over beef. Cover and cook on high setting one hour; reduce heat to low setting and cook 8 hours.

Add onion and green peppers; cover and cook on low setting one more hour. Remove beef and vegetables from slow cooker; shred beef with 2 forks. Serve beef mixture on warmed tortillas with desired garnishes. Serves 4.

Shelly Livingston
Shamrock, TX

tasty tailgating

Serve up hot & tasty sandwich fixin's at your next tailgating party…right out of a slow cooker! Plug it into a power inverter that uses your car battery to power appliances.

Swiss Steak

Smothered in tomatoes and onions, this comfort dish is finished with a gravy on top. Rice or mashed potatoes are a must to soak up the gravy.

2 lbs. boneless beef round steak, cut into 6 serving pieces
1.1-oz. pkg. beefy onion soup mix
½ t. salt
¼ t. pepper
3 c. onion, sliced
28-oz. can diced tomatoes, undrained
3 T. all-purpose flour
1 c. water

Place steak in a 5-quart slow cooker. Sprinkle soup mix, salt and pepper over steak; arrange onion slices on top. Top with tomatoes. Cover and cook on high setting one hour; reduce heat to low setting and cook 6 hours.

Remove steak and vegetables from slow cooker, reserving broth. Mix together flour and water; add to broth in slow cooker, stirring until thickened. Spoon gravy over steak to serve. Makes 4 to 6 servings.

Jean Carter
Rockledge, FL

terrific tomatoes

Add zest to a soup or stew…or other favorite recipe. Just choose a seasoned variety of canned diced tomatoes.

Just Perfect Sloppy Joes

A staple of easy weeknight cooking, these sandwiches will be ready and waiting for hungry family members at suppertime. Try a side of sweet potato fries.

3 lbs. ground beef, browned and
    drained
1 onion, finely chopped
1 green pepper, chopped
28-oz. can tomato sauce
¾ c. catsup

3 T. Worcestershire sauce
1 t. chili powder
½ t. black pepper
½ t. garlic powder
8 sandwich buns, split

Combine all ingredients except sandwich buns in a 5-quart slow cooker. Cover and cook on low setting 4 hours. Serve on sandwich buns. Serves 8.

Amy Wrightsel
Louisville, KY

"This recipe is very special to me. It brings back memories of my aunt and me puttering around in the kitchen trying to figure out just what it needed to be right."

Amy

Favorite Caramel Apples

For a special treat, press warm caramel apples into chopped peanuts, candy-coated chocolates, candy corn or red cinnamon candies.

2 (14-oz.) pkgs. caramels,
   unwrapped
¼ c. water

½ t. cinnamon
8 wooden skewers
8 apples

Combine caramels, water and cinnamon in a 3-quart oval slow cooker. Cover and cook on high setting one to 1½ hours, stirring every 20 minutes.

Insert skewers into apples. Reduce heat to low setting; dip apples into hot caramel and turn to coat, scraping excess caramel from bottom of apples. Place on greased wax paper to cool. Makes 8.

Graceann Frederico
Irondequoit, NY

chocolate-drizzled caramel apples

Make caramel apples extra special! Place semi-sweet chocolate chips in a plastic zipping bag. Microwave briefly on high until chocolate melts; then snip off a small corner of the bag and drizzle over apples.

Slow-Cooker Caramel Apple Delight

Top this sweet, gooey delight with vanilla ice cream or sweetened whipped cream. It easily reheats in the microwave…if there are leftovers. Cook on high heat, stirring at one-minute intervals.

½ c. apple juice
7-oz. pkg. caramels, unwrapped (26)
1 t. vanilla extract

½ t. cinnamon
⅓ c. creamy peanut butter
4 tart apples, cored, peeled and sliced

Combine apple juice, caramels, vanilla and cinnamon in a 4-quart slow cooker. Add peanut butter; mix well. Add apples; cover and cook on low setting 5 hours. Stir thoroughly; cover and cook on low setting one more hour. Serves 4.

Shelley Turner
Boise, ID

Sugared Walnuts

Not only are these walnuts a tasty treat to keep around, they send a spicy aroma throughout the house while cooking.

4½ c. walnut halves	1½ t. cinnamon
⅓ c. butter, melted	¼ t. ground cloves
½ c. powdered sugar	¼ t. ground ginger

Preheat a 3-quart slow cooker on high setting 15 minutes. Add walnuts and butter, stirring to mix well. Add powdered sugar; mix until coated evenly. Cover and cook on high setting 15 minutes; reduce heat to low setting and cook, uncovered, 3 hours or until nuts are coated with a crisp glaze, stirring occasionally.

Transfer nuts to a serving bowl, using a slotted spoon. Combine spices in a small bowl and sprinkle over nuts, stirring to coat evenly. Cool before serving. Store in an airtight container. Makes 4½ cups.

Connie Fortune
Covington, OH

food gift

Fill a Chinese take-out container with these yummy walnuts…always a welcomed gift!

Fudgy Pudding Cake

Warm, gooey and chocolatey are the words that best describe this sensational dessert! Ice cream is a favorite topping but the cake stands by itself just as well.

18.25-oz. pkg. devil's food
    cake mix
3.9-oz. pkg. instant chocolate
    pudding mix
16-oz. container sour cream
¾ c. oil

4 eggs
1 c. water
6-oz. pkg. semi-sweet chocolate
    chips
vanilla ice cream

Beat first 6 ingredients at low speed with an electric mixer 30 seconds or until blended. Beat at medium speed 2 minutes. Stir in chocolate chips. Pour into a lightly greased 4-quart round slow cooker.

Cover and cook on low setting 4 hours or until set around the edges but still soft in the center. Turn off slow cooker and let stand 20 to 30 minutes; do not lift lid until ready to serve. Serve with vanilla ice cream. Serves 8 to 10.

Carol McMillan
Catawba, VA

"This is scrumpdelicious! A friend brought it to the last 2 covered-dish dinners at our church...it disappeared very quickly!"

Carol

fancy dessert

Spoon generous portions of a warm, gooey dessert into stemmed glasses and dollop with whipped topping…a sweet ending that your guests will long remember!

Creamy Rice Pudding

1 pt. half-and-half
3 eggs
⅔ c. sugar
2 t. vanilla extract

1½ c. cooked rice
¾ c. raisins
½ t. ground nutmeg
½ t. cinnamon

Beat half-and-half, eggs, sugar and vanilla in a mixing bowl at medium speed with an electric mixer; stir in rice and remaining ingredients. Pour mixture into a greased 3-quart oval slow cooker. Cover and cook on high setting 30 minutes; stir well. Cover, reduce heat to low setting and cook 2½ hours. Stir well before serving. Serves 8 to 10.

Shelley Sparks
Amarillo, TX

easy clean-up

For easy clean-up, spray the crock of your slow cooker with non-stick vegetable spray before adding ingredients.

Texas 2-Step Apple Crisp

(pictured on page 162)

The slow cooker tenderizes these apples while creating a perfectly crisp topping...resulting in a grand finale for any meal.

6 cooking apples, cored, peeled
   and sliced
1½ c. all-purpose flour
1 c. brown sugar, packed
1 T. cinnamon
½ t. ground nutmeg

¼ t. ground ginger
½ c. butter, softened
Garnishes: vanilla ice cream,
   whipped topping, maraschino
   cherries

Arrange apple slices in a lightly greased 4- to 5-quart oval slow cooker; set aside.

Combine flour and next 5 ingredients in a bowl; mix well. Sprinkle flour mixture over apples, pressing down lightly. Cover and cook on low setting 5 hours or until apples are tender. Garnish with your favorite toppings. Makes 6 to 8 servings.

Jennifer Swartz
Smithville, TX

"So tasty, no need to dress it up, but a dollop of whipped cream dusted with cinnamon is a scrumptious topper!"

Jennifer

Unbelievable Caramel Pie

Two ingredients are all it takes to create this sinfully rich pie!

2 (14-oz.) cans sweetened
    condensed milk
9-inch graham cracker crust

Garnishes: whipped topping,
    mini semi-sweet chocolate
    chips

Pour condensed milk into a lightly greased one-quart slow cooker. Cover and cook on low setting 4 hours, stirring every 30 minutes. Pour into crust and chill. Garnish, if desired. Makes 6 to 8 servings.

Judy Collins
Nashville, TN

"Here in Nashville, one of the country clubs always served the most delicious caramel pie. This is such an easy way to get that wonderful caramel taste!"

Judy

make mine mini

Mini slow cookers are terrific for making sauces, melting chocolate and making this pie...keep one on hand.

Hearty Turkey Chili,
page 211, and Grilled Gouda
Sandwiches, page 219

soup & sandwich sensations

Served together or separately, soups & sandwiches are the ultimate in comfort foods. Nothing soothes the soul more than a bowlful of Chicken-Tortellini Soup (page 205). And for those brisk autumn nights, invite friends over for Hearty Turkey Chili (page 211)...it's perfect with a side of your favorite cornbread. Don't reserve sandwiches for lunch only...they're just the right choice when time's tight at night. From old favorites like Creamy Tuna Melt (page 225) to our version of a grown-up grilled cheese (page 219), we have the supper solution for you.

Chilled Cantaloupe Soup

When the weather turns warmer, look to refreshing chilled soups like this one for lunch or a light starter with supper.

1 cantaloupe, peeled, seeded
  and cubed
2 c. orange juice, divided

1 T. lime juice
¼ to ½ t. cinnamon
Optional: fresh mint sprigs

Combine cantaloupe and ½ cup orange juice in a blender or food processor. Cover and process until smooth. Transfer to a large bowl; stir in lime juice, cinnamon and remaining orange juice. Cover and chill at least one hour. Garnish with mint, if desired. Makes about 6 servings.

Jacqueline Kurtz
Reading, PA

choosing melons

Look for heirloom fruits & vegetables at the farmers' market…old-timers that Grandma knew and loved. To select the best melon, shake it and listen for the rattle of seeds. Pick one with a soft stem end and a light yellow ridged or smooth outer shell; avoid those with a green cast.

Yellow Squash Soup

Serve this soup hot or cold. When serving it cold, substitute vanilla yogurt for plain yogurt for just the right flavor...and a touch of sweetness.

1 yellow squash, sliced
1 onion, sliced
14½-oz. can chicken broth

pepper to taste
⅛ c. plain yogurt

Combine squash, onion and broth in a medium stockpot; cook over medium-high heat 15 minutes.

Add squash mixture, pepper and yogurt to a blender or food processor; process until smooth. Return mixture to pan and heat until warm. Makes 2 servings.

Roxanne Bixby
West Franklin, NH

soup & bread!

Pick up a loaf of freshly baked bread at your local bakery or grocery store the next time you plan on soup for supper. When warmed slightly in the oven and topped with butter, it's heavenly!

Chicken-Tortellini Soup

Substitute this version with cheese tortellini for ordinary chicken noodle soup. It's just as easy and equally soothing.

1 lb. boneless, skinless chicken
    breasts, cooked and cubed
9-oz. pkg. cheese tortellini,
    uncooked
46-oz. can chicken broth
1 c. carrots, peeled and chopped

½ c. onion, chopped
½ c. celery, sliced
½ t. dried thyme
¼ t. pepper
1 bay leaf

Combine all ingredients in a stockpot; bring to a boil over medium heat. Reduce heat, cover and simmer until tortellini is tender. Discard bay leaf. Serves 6.

Chris McCain
Mosinee, WI

pick-me-ups

A pot of chicken soup and a cheery bouquet of posies are sure pick-me-ups for a friend who is feeling under the weather.

South Carolina Gumbo

Okra imparts a rich flavor to the gumbo and aids in its thickening as it simmers. It's also what gives this gumbo its Southern name.

1 T. olive oil
1 onion, chopped
1 stalk celery, sliced
½ green pepper, chopped
2 c. boneless, skinless chicken breasts, cubed
2 c. okra, chopped
2 (14½-oz.) cans chicken broth

1 c. water
14½-oz. can diced tomatoes
½ t. garlic powder
2 t. Cajun seasoning
1 t. salt
½ t. black pepper
1 c. instant rice, uncooked

Heat oil in a stockpot. Add onion, celery and green pepper; sauté over medium-high heat until tender. Add chicken and remaining ingredients except rice; bring to a boil. Reduce heat and simmer, covered, 15 minutes or until chicken is done. Add rice and simmer 15 more minutes. Makes 10 cups.

Rachel Reilly
Columbia, SC

Cajun seasoning

If you don't have any Cajun seasoning on hand, simply stir together ½ teaspoon each of black pepper, white pepper, garlic powder, onion powder, cayenne pepper and paprika.

Lentil-Barley Vegetable Stew

Chock-full of vegetables, herbs, lentils and barley, this stew is bursting with flavor and is so good for you!

4 carrots, peeled and diced
2 leeks, diced
2 stalks celery, diced
2 zucchini, diced
1 onion, chopped
½ c. okra, sliced
1 c. dried lentils

½ c. pearled barley, uncooked
6 to 7 c. vegetable broth
1 c. fresh basil, torn
¼ c. olive oil
1 T. garlic, minced
1 t. dried thyme

Combine all ingredients in a stockpot. Bring to a boil; reduce heat to medium and simmer until lentils and barley are tender, about 30 minutes. Serves 4.

Carrie Knotts
Kalispell, MT

"When my grandmother 'MaMaw Lou' passed away, all I wanted were her cookbooks. I found this recipe in one of them and just love it."

Carrie

kitchen garden

Turn an old wagon wheel into a mini herb garden right outside your kitchen door. Plant basil, thyme, marjoram, chives, sage and other fragrant herbs between the spokes.

Lillian's Beef Stew

Tapioca is used to thicken this comfort-food dish. If you don't have any on hand, substitute an equal amount of flour.

2 lbs. stew beef, cubed
2 potatoes, peeled and quartered
3 stalks celery, diced
4 carrots, peeled and thickly
   sliced
2 onions, quartered
2 c. cocktail vegetable juice

⅓ c. quick-cooking tapioca,
   uncooked
1 T. sugar
1 T. salt
½ t. dried basil
¼ t. pepper

Arrange beef and vegetables in a 5-quart round slow cooker. Combine remaining ingredients; pour into slow cooker. Cover and cook on high setting one hour; reduce heat to low setting and cook 7 hours. Serves 8.

Nancy Dynes
Goose Creek, SC

"My mother made this for us when we were small children and now I make it for my own family. It's a wonderful dinner to come home to on a cold day."

Nancy

Black Bean Chili

Make up a batch of cheese quesadillas to go alongside this Southwestern-flavored chili. It's also good with corn or tortilla chips if time is tight.

1 t. oil
2 onions, chopped
2 cloves garlic, minced
4.5-oz. can diced green chiles, drained
2 t. chili powder

1 t. ground cumin
1 t. dried oregano
14½-oz. can diced tomatoes
1 c. water
2 (15-oz.) cans black beans, drained

Heat oil in a skillet; add onions and garlic and sauté until tender. Stir in chiles and remaining ingredients except beans; bring to a boil over medium heat. Reduce heat; simmer 10 minutes. Stir in beans; heat thoroughly. Makes 7 cups.

Sharon Velenosi
Garden Grove, CA

clever placecards

Having friends over for a Chili Supper? Create placecards in no time. Place a miniature pumpkin in a candy corn-filled ramekin. Slip copper wire that's been curled around a pencil over the pumpkin stem and then tuck in the placecard.

Hearty Turkey Chili

(pictured on page 200)

If you prefer, extra-lean ground beef can be substituted for the ground turkey.

1 lb. ground turkey, browned
1 onion, chopped
15½-oz. can kidney beans
15-oz. can corn, drained
1½ c. water
1 c. celery, chopped

1 T. chili powder
1 t. salt
14½-oz. can diced tomatoes
¼ t. pepper
Optional: shredded Cheddar
   cheese

Combine all ingredients except cheese in a stockpot. Bring mixture to a boil; cover, reduce heat and simmer until celery is tender, stirring occasionally. Spoon into bowls; top with shredded Cheddar cheese, if desired. Makes 4 to 6 servings.

Carla Marcinek
Huntington Beach, CA

"Make a pan of cornbread or a sheet of cornbread twists to enjoy on the side."

Carla

bread bowls

Scoop out the centers of small round bread loaves for bread bowls in a snap…it's convenient and extra special for serving hot soup or chili.

Cheeseburger Soup

All the ingredients of your favorite cheeseburger are included in this chunky soup.

2 c. potatoes, peeled and cubed
2 carrots, peeled and grated
1 onion, chopped
1 jalapeño pepper, seeded and
  chopped
1 clove garlic, minced
1½ c. water
1 T. beef bouillon granules
½ t. salt
1 lb. ground beef, browned and
  drained

2½ c. milk, divided
3 T. all-purpose flour
8-oz. pkg. pasteurized process
  cheese spread, cubed
Optional: ¼ to 1 t. cayenne
  pepper
Garnish: ½ lb. bacon, crisply
  cooked and crumbled

Combine first 8 ingredients in a large saucepan; bring to a boil over medium heat. Reduce heat and simmer until potatoes are tender. Stir in ground beef and 2 cups milk.

Whisk together flour and remaining milk in a small bowl until smooth; gradually whisk into soup. Bring to a boil; cook 2 minutes or until thick and bubbly, stirring constantly. Reduce heat; add cheese and stir until melted. Add cayenne pepper, if desired. Top with bacon just before serving. Makes 8 cups.

Lacy Mayfield
Earth, TX

"My son's favorite! When his first-grade class made recipe holders for Mothers' Day, he insisted that I put this recipe in the holder. Kids really do like this soup...the jalapeño doesn't taste hot when it's done."

Lacy

Seafood Bisque in a Snap

Thanks to convenience products, this bisque is ready in minutes.

¼ c. butter
1 onion, chopped
2 stalks celery, chopped
1 T. garlic, chopped
8-oz. pkg. imitation seafood pieces
15-oz. can potatoes, drained and diced
2 (12-oz.) cans evaporated milk
¼ c. water

10¾-oz. can cream of potato soup
10¾-oz. can cream of mushroom soup
10¾-oz. can cream of shrimp soup
10¾-oz. can Cheddar cheese soup
Optional: 2 T. sherry

Melt butter in a large Dutch oven over medium heat. Add onion, celery and garlic; cook until tender. Reduce heat and stir in seafood and potatoes; heat thoroughly.

Add milk, water and soups to Dutch oven, stirring until smooth; cook until thoroughly heated. Add sherry just before serving, if desired. Serves 4 to 6.

Diane Smith
Burlington, NJ

savory crackers

Treat yourself to crisp savory crackers with your next bowl of soup. Spread saltines with softened butter, then sprinkle with garlic powder, thyme, paprika or another favorite spice. Pop into a 350-degree oven for 3 to 6 minutes or just until golden.

Family Favorite Clam Chowder

This New England-style chowder will quickly become a favorite of your family, too. Save prep time by purchasing prechopped onion and celery from the produce section of your supermarket.

3 to 4 c. potatoes, peeled and
    cubed
1 c. onion, diced
1 c. celery, diced
6½-oz. can minced clams,
    drained and juice reserved
8-oz. bottle clam juice

¾ c. butter
¾ c. all-purpose flour
1 qt. half-and-half
½ t. sugar
1½ t. salt
⅛ t. pepper

Combine first 3 ingredients in a large saucepan; add reserved clam juice and bottled clam juice. Add just enough water to cover vegetables; bring to a boil over medium heat. Reduce heat; simmer, covered, 10 to 15 minutes or until vegetables are tender.

Melt butter in a separate saucepan over medium heat; whisk in flour and cook one minute. Add half-and-half, sugar, salt and pepper; cook over low heat 3 to 4 minutes, whisking until smooth. Stir into vegetable mixture; add clams and cook 5 minutes or until thoroughly heated. Serves 8.

Angie Whitmore
Farmington, UT

thoughtful touch

Pre-warmed soup bowls are oh-so simple to do. Just place bowls in a 250-degree oven as you put finishing touches on dinner. Then they'll be nice & warm when the soup's ready to serve.

Cobb Sandwiches

If you don't have time to fry bacon, bacon bits are convenient to use…just mix them with the blue cheese dressing.

2 T. blue cheese salad dressing
3 slices bread, toasted
1 leaf green leaf lettuce
3 thin slices tomato
6-oz. grilled boneless, skinless
   chicken breast, sliced

1 thinly sliced red onion
3 slices avocado
3 slices bacon, crisply cooked

Spread blue cheese dressing on one side of each slice of toasted bread. On the first slice of bread, layer lettuce, tomato and half of chicken on dressing; top with a second bread slice. Layer on onion, avocado, remaining chicken slices and bacon; top with remaining bread slice. Cut sandwich in half, securing each section with a toothpick. Makes 2 sandwich wedges.

Joyce Chizauskie
Vacaville, CA

Mark's Egg Salad Sandwiches

Keep hard-boiled eggs in the fridge to whip up quick sandwich spreads like this one. Hard-boiled eggs can be kept in the fridge up to one week.

6 eggs, hard-boiled, peeled and chopped
⅓ c. celery, finely chopped
⅓ c. onion, finely chopped
3 to 4 T. mayonnaise-type salad dressing
1 to 2 t. mustard
1 t. Worcestershire sauce
½ t. salt
¼ t. pepper
½ t. dry mustard
1 T. dill weed
1 loaf sliced bread

Mix all ingredients except bread in a small bowl; chill one hour. Spread mixture on bread. Makes 6 to 8 servings.

Connie Herek
Bay City, MI

creative serving trays

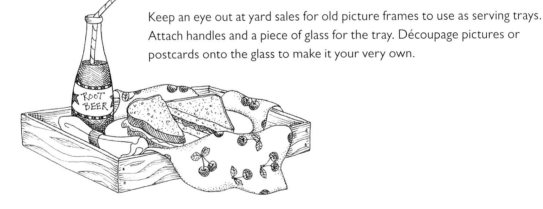

Keep an eye out at yard sales for old picture frames to use as serving trays. Attach handles and a piece of glass for the tray. Découpage pictures or postcards onto the glass to make it your very own.

Grilled Gouda Sandwiches

(pictured on page 200)

Good ol' grilled cheese takes on a grown-up flavor with Gouda cheese, Dijon mustard and garlic-rubbed country-style bread.

8 slices country-style bread
1 clove garlic, halved
4 t. Dijon mustard
8 slices Gouda cheese

2 T. butter, melted
⅛ t. cayenne pepper
⅛ t. black pepper

Rub one side of each slice of bread with garlic. Place 4 bread slices garlic-side down; top each bread slice with one teaspoon mustard and 2 slices Gouda. Place remaining bread slices, garlic-side up, on sandwich bottoms. Combine butter, cayenne pepper and black pepper in a small bowl; brush mixture over each side of sandwiches.

Cook sandwiches in an oven-proof skillet over medium-high heat about 2 minutes on each side or until golden. Place skillet in oven and bake at 400 degrees for 5 minutes or until cheese is melted. Slice sandwiches diagonally. Makes 4 sandwiches.

Tiffany Brinkley

make it special

Even a simple sandwich supper with family can be memorable when it's thoughtfully served. Use the good china, set out cloth napkins and a vase of fresh flowers... after all, who's more special than your family?

Muffuletta Sandwich

This New Orleans-inspired sandwich is similar to an Italian hero-style sandwich made with a variety of meats and cheese layered on a round loaf. But what makes it distinctively a muffuletta is the olive salad.

¾ c. green olives, chopped
¾ c. black olives, chopped
1 clove garlic, minced
⅓ c. chopped pimento
¼ c. fresh parsley, chopped
¾ t. dried oregano
¼ t. pepper
⅓ c. plus 1 T. olive oil, divided

1 round loaf Italian bread
½ lb. sliced honey ham
½ lb. sliced turkey
¼ lb. sliced Muenster cheese
Optional: mayonnaise-type
    salad dressing
8 to 10 dill pickle slices

Mix olives, garlic, pimento, herbs, pepper and ⅓ cup oil in a small bowl; set aside.

Cut loaf in half horizontally and hollow out the center. Brush cut side of bottom half with remaining oil; layer ham, turkey and cheese slices on top. Spread salad dressing between the layers, if desired. Top with pickle slices. Fill top half of loaf with the olive mixture; place bottom loaf on top and invert. Wrap tightly in plastic wrap and chill overnight. Let stand until loaf comes to room temperature; cut into wedges. Serves 6 to 8.

Kris Bailey
Conklin, NY

"This is one of my family's favorites. Try it with different cold cuts and cheeses...great with salami, Swiss and provolone."

Kris

Chicken Veggie Sandwiches

Ordinary grilled chicken sandwiches get a flavor punch with bell peppers, onion, provolone cheese and a sprinkling of red pepper flakes.

4 boneless, skinless chicken breasts, sliced into strips
2 T. oil
1 red pepper, sliced
1 green pepper, sliced
1 sweet onion, thinly sliced
13¼-oz. can mushroom stems and pieces, drained

salt and black pepper to taste
¼ t. red pepper flakes
6 sandwich rolls, sliced in half horizontally
6 slices provolone cheese

Brown chicken in oil in a skillet over medium-high heat; add peppers and onion slices and sauté until vegetables are tender. Stir in mushrooms, salt, black pepper and red pepper and heat thoroughly. Spoon warm chicken mixture onto bottom halves of rolls; top with slices of cheese and top halves of rolls. Serves 6.

Kristie Rigo
Friedens, PA

for the family on-the-run

If family members will be dining at different times, fix sandwiches ahead of time, wrap in aluminum foil and refrigerate. Pop them into a toaster oven or under a broiler to heat…fresh, tasty and ready when you are!

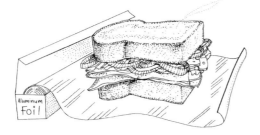

Chicken Salad Croissants

This isn't your ordinary chicken salad. This version stirs in raisins, almonds and dried cranberries. These sandwiches are a treat for a quick supper or a casual weekend lunch.

2 c. cooked chicken, cubed
⅓ c. celery, diced
¼ c. raisins
¼ c. dried cranberries
¼ c. sliced almonds
⅔ c. mayonnaise
⅛ t. pepper

1 T. fresh parsley, minced
1 t. mustard
1 T. lemon juice
4 croissants, split in half
   horizontally
4 lettuce leaves

    Combine all ingredients except croissants and lettuce leaves in a large mixing bowl; mix well. Cover and chill 2 to 3 hours. Spoon about ¾ cup mixture on the bottom half of each croissant; add a lettuce leaf and the top croissant half. Makes 4 sandwiches.

Arlene Smulski
Lyons, IL

deli-roasted chicken

Pick up a roasted chicken at the deli for 2 meals in one. Serve it hot the first night, then slice or cube the rest to become the delicious start of a sandwich, soup or salad supper the next night.

Creamy Tuna Melt

This old-fashioned favorite is given a new twist by combining cottage cheese and mayonnaise with tuna and sautéed celery and onion. The result? A creamy mixture that's heaped on top of English muffin halves and then broiled with American cheese...yummy!

3 stalks celery, diced
1 onion, diced
12-oz. can tuna, drained
½ c. cottage cheese
½ c. mayonnaise

¼ t. garlic salt
⅛ t. sugar
4 English muffins, split and
    toasted
8 slices American cheese

Spray a skillet with non-stick vegetable spray. Add celery and onion and sauté over medium-high heat until tender. Reduce heat to low; add tuna and next 4 ingredients and cook until thoroughly heated, stirring frequently. Remove from heat.

Place toasted muffins, cut-side up, on a broiler pan. Spread with tuna mixture and top with cheese slices. Broil until cheese melts; serve immediately. Makes 8 open-faced sandwiches.

Cindy Atkins
Vancouver, WA

Aloha Burgers

Grilled pineapple slices top these burgers…giving you a taste of the tropics with each bite.

8-oz. can pineapple slices,
   drained and juice reserved
¾ c. teriyaki sauce
1 lb. ground beef
1 T. butter, softened

4 hamburger buns, split
4 slices Swiss cheese
4 slices bacon, crisply cooked
4 leaves lettuce
1 red onion, sliced

Stir together reserved pineapple juice and teriyaki sauce in a small bowl. Place pineapple slices and 3 tablespoons reserved juice mixture in a plastic zipping bag. Turn to coat; set aside.

Shape ground beef into 4 patties and spoon remaining juice mixture over top; set aside. Spread butter on cut sides of buns; set aside. Grill patties over medium-high heat (350 to 400 degrees) to desired doneness, turning to cook on both sides. Place buns on grill, cut-side down, to toast lightly. Remove pineapple slices from plastic bag; place on grill and cook one minute on each side or until lightly golden. Serve burgers on buns topped with pineapple, cheese, bacon, lettuce and onion. Serves 4.

Jo Ann
Gooseberry Patch

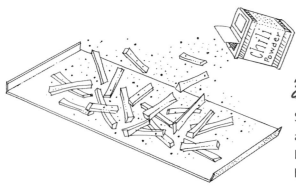

zesty French fries

Spray frozen fries with non-stick olive oil spray and sprinkle with your favorite spice blend, such as Italian, Cajun or steakhouse seasoning. Spread on a baking sheet and bake as directed.

Steakhouse Sandwiches

Bring that steakhouse flavor into your home with servings of these hearty steak sandwiches.

2 c. cooked beef flank steak, diced
5 T. mayonnaise, divided
1 T. Dijon mustard
2 T. red onion, chopped
2 T. dill pickle, chopped
salt and pepper to taste
8 thick slices country-style bread
4 leaves romaine lettuce
1 tomato, cut into 8 slices

Combine steak, 2 tablespoons mayonnaise, mustard, onion and pickle in a medium bowl; add salt and pepper. Spread one side of each bread slice with remaining mayonnaise. Divide steak mixture among 4 slices of bread; top each with a lettuce leaf, 2 tomato slices and a second slice of bread, mayonnaise-side down. Slice sandwiches diagonally. Makes 4 sandwiches.

John Alexander
New Britain, CT

leftover genius

Crispy potato pancakes are a great way to use leftover mashed potatoes. Stir an egg yolk and some minced onion into 2 cups mashed potatoes. Form into patties and fry in butter until golden. They're a tasty accompaniment to these steak sandwiches.

Italian Meatball Subs

Look for packages of frozen, cooked meatballs in your grocer's freezer if you don't have time to make your own.

1 onion, sliced
½ c. green pepper, sliced
2 T. water
8-oz. can pizza sauce

24 meatballs, cooked
4 Italian hard rolls, sliced and
    hollowed out
½ c. shredded provolone cheese

"Pass any leftover sauce for dipping."

Dana

Cook onion, pepper and water, covered, in a large saucepan over medium heat just until tender; drain. Stir in pizza sauce and meatballs; cook until hot and bubbly. Fill each roll with 6 meatballs; top with sauce mixture. Sprinkle with cheese and add roll tops. Place sandwiches in a lightly greased 13"x9" baking pan. Bake at 400 degrees for 10 to 15 minutes or until bread is crusty and cheese is melted. Serves 4.

Dana Thompson
Gooseberry Patch

Grilled Cuban Sandwiches

Roast pork is layered with ham and cheese and then lightly toasted inside buttered rolls. It's a Caribbean favorite...and guaranteed to become a favorite of yours, too!

4 submarine rolls, split
4 t. mustard
⅓ lb. roast pork, thinly sliced
4 slices Swiss cheese

⅓ lb. deli ham, thinly sliced
dill pickle slices
1 T. butter, softened

Spread rolls with mustard; layer bottoms of rolls with pork, cheese, ham and pickles. Add tops of rolls; lightly spread outside surface of rolls with butter. Grill on a hot griddle over medium heat until lightly toasted and cheese is melted. Makes 4 sandwiches.

Beth Kramer
Port Saint Lucie, FL

quick & easy side

Slice fresh tomatoes in half and sprinkle with minced garlic, Italian seasoning and grated Parmesan cheese. Broil 5 minutes or until tomatoes are tender... scrumptious!

Scrumptious Sandwich Loaves

You'll feed quite a crowd with these sandwiches…and they're easy to make ahead, too!

2 loaves Italian bread
8-oz. pkg. cream cheese, softened
1 c. shredded Cheddar cheese
¾ c. green onions, chopped
¼ c. mayonnaise

1 T. Worcestershire sauce
1 lb. sliced deli ham
1 lb. sliced roast beef
¼ to ½ c. dill pickle slices

Cut loaves in half lengthwise; hollow out halves. Set aside.

Combine cheeses, green onions, mayonnaise and Worcestershire sauce; spread over both halves of bread. Layer ham, beef and pickles on bottom halves of bread; press on top halves. Wrap in plastic wrap; chill at least 2 hours. Cut into 1½- to 2-inch slices. Serves 12 to 14.

Dee Ann Ice
Delaware, OH

suppertime picnic

If busy kids can't get home for dinner, take it to them. Pack a tailgating basket and enjoy picnicking with them at the ballpark. Be sure to pack extra for hungry team members.

Marinated Tomatoes,
page 247

speedy
sides & salads

From go-to dishes like Creamed Corn (page 238) to an exciting new way with cauliflower (page 237), you'll discover savory & sweet sides to deliciously round out your meal. For super salad selections, don't miss Blue Crab Salad (page 262) or Orange-Wild Rice Chicken Salad (page 265)…either is perfect for lunch or a light supper. And surprise everyone with Creamy Pretzel Salad (page 250)… we'll let you decide whether to begin or end your meal with this favorite.

Escalloped Apples

This sweet side pairs well with any pork or ham dish. Granny Smith apples are a favorite choice for this recipe.

10 c. tart apples, cored, peeled
   and sliced
⅓ c. sugar
2 T. cornstarch

1 t. cinnamon
¼ t. ground nutmeg
2 T. chilled butter, sliced

Place apples in a 2½-quart microwave-safe bowl; set aside. Combine sugar, cornstarch, cinnamon and nutmeg; sprinkle over apples. Toss gently to coat; dot with butter.

Cover and microwave on high 15 minutes or until apples are tender, stirring every 5 minutes. Serves 8 to 10.

Alison O'Keeffe
Westerville, OH

Garlic Roasted Asparagus

Roasting really brings out the flavor of fresh asparagus. Once you've tried this quick & easy method, you'll cook it this way time & time again.

1 lb. asparagus, trimmed
1 T. olive oil
3 cloves garlic, pressed

¼ t. salt
¼ t. pepper

Toss together all ingredients; arrange in a single layer on a lightly greased baking sheet. Bake at 450 degrees for 8 minutes or until tender. Serves 4.

Jeanne Calkins
Midland, MI

Green Beans with Bacon & Garlic

Look for packages of ready-to-eat trimmed fresh green beans in your produce section. The beans can be microwaved right in their bags...a big time saver.

6 slices bacon
¼ c. butter
2 t. garlic, minced
½ t. salt

¼ t. pepper
1 lb. green beans, cut into
    bite-size pieces and cooked

Cook bacon in a skillet over medium heat until crisp; drain. Crumble bacon and return to skillet.

Add butter, garlic, salt and pepper to skillet; cook until butter is melted. Place beans in a serving bowl; toss with bacon mixture and serve immediately. Makes 4 servings.

Diane Stout
Zeeland, MI

"I invented this recipe so my daughter would enjoy eating green beans. It's good made with either fresh or frozen beans."

Diane

potluck dinner

Invite the neighbors over for a casual dinner and let everyone help in the preparations. It's a terrific way to swap and try new recipes.

French-Fried Cauliflower

The buttery, crisp coating on the cauliflower adds flavor and is a sure-fire way to get children of all ages to eat their vegetables…and enjoy them!

1 head cauliflower, cut into
    flowerets
3 eggs, beaten

1 sleeve round buttery crackers,
    crushed
oil for deep frying

Dip cauliflower into eggs; coat with cracker crumbs. Pour oil to a depth of ½ inch in a heavy skillet; heat oil to 375 degrees. Fry cauliflower, in batches, 3 minutes or until golden; drain on paper towels. Makes 6 to 8 servings.

Roseann Haley
Cutler, IN

"Kids love it and will remember it forever!"

Roseann

Creamed Corn

If you have a little extra time, use fresh corn on the cob...it's at its peak May through September. Just use the liquid from the corn instead of the milk called for in the recipe.

1 c. canned corn
½ t. milk
2 T. sugar
2 slices bacon, crisply cooked,
   crumbled and drippings
   reserved

3 T. all-purpose flour
½ c. water
salt and pepper to taste

Combine corn and milk in a medium bowl; add sugar. Place corn mixture and bacon drippings in a large skillet. Whisk together flour and water in a measuring cup until smooth. Add enough additional water to the measuring cup to equal one cup. Add flour mixture to corn and stir over medium heat until mixture is thickened. Add salt and pepper to taste; cook 10 to 15 minutes. Serves 4 to 6.

Sherri Smith
Ravenna, OH

restaurant style

Look for old restaurant serving dishes at flea markets and antique shops...they're roomy enough to hold the largest family recipes.

Garlic Deviled Eggs

"Deviled" refers to highly seasoned food. The hot, spicy flavor in some deviled eggs may come from ingredients in the filling like mustard, cayenne pepper, horseradish or hot pepper sauce. These eggs have a mild flavor but are a favorite staple at potlucks & picnics throughout the country.

6 eggs, hard-boiled and peeled
⅓ c. mayonnaise
½ to 1 t. mustard
1 t. pickle relish

1 onion, chopped
1 clove garlic, minced
⅛ t. salt
Garnish: paprika

Slice eggs in half lengthwise; remove yolks and set egg white halves aside.

Combine yolks, mayonnaise and next 5 ingredients; mix well. Spoon yolk mixture evenly into egg white halves; sprinkle with paprika, if desired. Makes 12.

Jennifer Eveland
Blandon, PA

quick tip

Whip up deviled eggs in no time by combining ingredients in a plastic zipping bag instead of a bowl. Blend by squeezing the bag, then snip off a corner and pipe the filling into the egg white halves.

Fresh Tomato & Basil Linguine

If ripe garden tomatoes are out of season, roma or cherry tomatoes are good substitutes.

1½ lbs. tomatoes, finely
    chopped
3 cloves garlic, minced
1 red pepper, chopped
1 bunch fresh basil, torn

½ c. olive oil
1 t. salt
¼ t. freshly ground black pepper
16-oz. pkg. linguine, cooked
Garnish: grated Parmesan cheese

Stir together tomatoes, garlic, red pepper and basil in a large bowl; drizzle with oil. Sprinkle with salt and black pepper; mix well and toss with hot cooked linguine. Sprinkle with Parmesan cheese, if desired. Serves 6 to 8.

Vickie
Gooseberry Patch

pasta tonight

If pasta is on the menu tonight, put a big pot of water on to boil as soon as you arrive home…it'll be boiling in no time.

Savory Orzo Dish

Orzo is actually tiny, rice-shaped pasta. Flavored with garlic and herb soup mix, it's a good pick to complement your favorite main dish.

2 T. butter
2 cloves garlic, minced
¼ t. salt
1½ c. orzo pasta, uncooked
1½-oz. pkg. savory herb
   soup mix

4 c. water
8-oz. pkg. sliced mushrooms
2 T. fresh parsley, chopped

Melt butter in a skillet over medium heat; add garlic, salt and pasta and heat until garlic is golden, stirring constantly. Stir in soup mix and water; simmer 10 minutes. Add mushrooms; simmer 10 more minutes or until liquid is absorbed. Stir in parsley. Serves 2 to 4.

Bev Eckert
Jonesboro, AR

Sweet Brown Rice

Substitute dried apricots, dates, figs or prune pieces for the dried cranberries to add a variety of flavors to this easy side.

14-oz. pkg. instant brown rice,
   uncooked
½ c. sweetened dried cranberries
½ c. sunflower seeds

2 T. orange marmalade
1 T. spicy mustard
1½ t. prepared horseradish
1 T. honey

Prepare rice according to package directions, adding cranberries and sunflower seeds as rice simmers.

Meanwhile, microwave marmalade in a microwave-safe bowl on high 10 seconds. Combine marmalade, mustard, horseradish and honey in a medium bowl; toss with cooked rice. Serves 9.

Natalie Holdren
Overland Park, KS

Loaded Baked Potato Casserole

All your favorite baked potato toppings are mixed together to create one fabulous casserole that's bursting with flavor. Save time by microwaving your potatoes on high about 15 to 20 minutes...you can even leave the peels on.

3 lbs. potatoes, peeled, cubed
    and boiled
16-oz. container sour cream
½ c. butter, melted
8-oz. pkg. shredded sharp
    Cheddar cheese

5 slices bacon, crisply cooked
    and crumbled
Optional: shredded sharp
    Cheddar cheese

*"In a word...
scrumptious!"*

Shannon

Mash together potatoes, sour cream and butter. Spoon mixture into a lightly greased 13"x9" baking dish; stir in cheese and bacon. Top with additional cheese, if desired. Bake at 350 degrees for 20 minutes or until thoroughly heated and cheese is melted. Serves 6 to 8.

Shannon Franklin
Hartsville, SC

cooking down memory lane

Use Mom's (or Grandma's) vintage baking dishes from the 1950's to serve up casseroles with sweet memories. If you don't have any of hers, keep an eye open at tag sales and thrift stores...you may find the very same kind of dishes she used.

Pineapple-Topped Sweet Potatoes

For individual servings, place sweet potato mixture into 6-ounce ungreased ramekins. Halve the Pineapple Topping and sprinkle evenly on top of sweet potatoes; bake as directed below.

2 c. sweet potatoes, peeled,
   boiled and mashed
¼ t. salt
¼ c. butter or margarine,
   softened

1 c. sugar
2 eggs, beaten
¼ c. milk
1 t. vanilla extract
Pineapple Topping

"My family won't eat sweet potatoes any other way!"

Linda

Combine all ingredients except Pineapple Topping; spoon into an ungreased 2-quart casserole dish. Spoon on Pineapple Topping; bake at 350 degrees for 30 minutes. Serves 8.

Pineapple Topping:

¼ c. all-purpose flour
½ c. sugar
1 egg, beaten
¼ c. butter or margarine,
   softened

8-oz. can crushed pineapple,
   drained

Combine flour and sugar; stir in egg and butter. Fold in pineapple; mix well.

Linda Littlejohn
Greensboro, NC

Lemon-Rice Pilaf

This version of pilaf stands out with vermicelli cooked with the rice. When zesting, be careful to remove only the colored skin of the lemon and not the white pith beneath, which tends to be very bitter.

2 T. butter
½ c. long-grain rice, uncooked
½ c. vermicelli, uncooked and
    broken into 1-inch pieces

1¾ c. chicken broth
1 T. lemon zest
1 T. fresh parsley, chopped

Melt butter in a saucepan over medium heat; add rice and vermicelli and cook until golden. Add broth and bring to a boil. Reduce heat; cover and simmer 15 to 20 minutes. Stir in lemon zest and parsley. Serves 4.

Esther Robinson
Brownsville, TX

shear genius

Kitchen shears are practical and oh-so easy to use. Use them to snip fresh herbs, cut canned tomatoes right in the can and cut the ends off fresh green beans. Just remember to wash them with soap and water after each use.

Marinated Tomatoes

(pictured on page 232)

When in season, vine-ripened tomatoes are the tastiest paired with the fresh herbs in this dish.

1 clove garlic, minced
1 t. fresh thyme, chopped
¼ c. green onions, chopped
¼ c. fresh parsley, minced
1 t. salt

¼ t. pepper
6 tomatoes, thickly sliced
¼ t. balsamic vinegar
⅓ c. oil

Combine first 6 ingredients; sprinkle over tomatoes. Set aside.

Stir together vinegar and oil; pour over tomatoes. Cover and refrigerate at least 2 hours. Mix gently before serving. Serves 10.

Mary Baker
Fountain, NC

"Absolutely delicious with tomatoes freshly picked from the garden."

Mary

Zucchini-Corn Sauté

Visit your local farmers' market to select the fresh vegetables and herbs needed for this side dish.

2 T. butter
1 zucchini, chopped
1 onion, chopped
1 jalapeño pepper, diced
⅛ t. salt
⅛ t. pepper

garlic powder to taste
2 to 3 ears corn, husked and
    kernels cut off
Optional: fresh cilantro,
    sour cream

Melt butter in a skillet. Add zucchini and next 5 ingredients; sauté over medium-high heat until vegetables are tender. Stir in corn and sauté 3 more minutes or until corn is tender. Garnish with fresh cilantro and sour cream, if desired. Serves 4.

Mindy Aragon
Greeley, CO

"We like to wrap this tasty dish in flour tortillas."

Mindy

7-Fruit Salad

The soothing taste of this chilled fruit salad will be welcome during the heat of summer.

½ c. lime juice
½ c. water
½ c. sugar
2 nectarines, peeled and thinly
    sliced
1 banana, thinly sliced
1 pt. blueberries

1 pt. strawberries, hulled and
    sliced
1½ c. watermelon, scooped
    into balls
1½ c. green grapes
1 kiwi, peeled and chopped

Whisk together lime juice, water and sugar in a medium bowl until sugar dissolves; add nectarines and bananas, stirring to coat. Combine blueberries and remaining 4 ingredients in a 2½-quart glass serving bowl; add nectarine mixture, gently tossing to mix. Cover and refrigerate one hour. Serves 8 to 10.

Laurie Parks
Westerville, OH

"This salad is always a hit at summer get-togethers...and no one believes how easy it is!"

Laurie

salads to go

Serving juicy, fruit-filled salads outdoors can sometimes be tricky, so why not spoon individual servings into one-pint, wide-mouth Mason jars? Secure the lids, and when it's serving time, friends will find the tasty fruit salad, and the juices, stay right inside the jars.

Creamy Pretzel Salad

Pretzels add crunch to this sweet pineapple salad.

½ c. butter
1 c. sugar, divided
3 c. pretzels, broken
8-oz. pkg. cream cheese, softened

8-oz. container frozen whipped topping, thawed
20-oz. can pineapple tidbits, drained

Melt butter in a saucepan over medium heat; stir in ½ cup sugar until dissolved. Place pretzels in an ungreased 13"x9" baking pan; pour butter mixture over top. Bake at 350 degrees for 10 minutes; let cool.

Mix together remaining sugar, cream cheese, whipped topping and pineapple; stir in pretzel pieces. Chill. Serves 10 to 12.

Wendy Gover
Fort Collins, CO

Easy Summer Broccoli Salad

Five ingredients are all it takes to toss together this dish. Use prepackaged broccoli flowerets to save time. You'll find them in the produce section of your supermarket.

2 c. broccoli flowerets
1 c. seedless red grapes
¾ c. coleslaw dressing

½ c. sweetened dried cranberries
¼ c. sunflower seeds

Mix together all ingredients, tossing well. Serves 4.

Lori Pearson
Orem, UT

Cauliflower Salad

Sugar is combined with salad dressing and Parmesan cheese to give this salad a savory-sweet flavor.

1 head lettuce, torn
1 to 2 heads cauliflower, chopped
1 lb. bacon, crisply cooked and
    crumbled
½ c. onion, finely chopped

2 c. mayonnaise-type salad
    dressing
¼ c. grated Parmesan cheese
¼ c. sugar

Toss together first 4 ingredients; set aside.
Combine salad dressing, cheese and sugar; fold into lettuce mixture.
Cover and refrigerate until ready to serve. Serves 8.

Barb Brosseau
Tinley Park, IL

tossed salad

Serving salad alongside dinner tonight? Tear greens and place in a large plastic bowl with a tight-fitting lid. Add any favorite salad toppers and dressing, then tighten the lid and shake to toss.

Iceberg & Thousand Island Salad

Simple iceberg lettuce wedges take center stage in this classic salad that's drizzled with a homemade dressing.

1 c. mayonnaise
⅓ c. chili sauce
1 T. green olives, chopped
1 T. pimento, chopped

1 egg, hard-boiled, peeled and
  separated
1 head lettuce, cut into 6 wedges

Combine first 4 ingredients in a jar. Chop egg yolk and add to mayonnaise mixture, reserving egg white for another recipe. Blend well; chill.

To serve, arrange lettuce wedges on individual plates; divide dressing among the wedges. Serves 6.

April Jacobs
Loveland, CO

Farmer's Wife Salad

We're guessing that this salad got its name because it's made from ingredients readily available in the garden…and pantry.

1 head broccoli, chopped
1 head romaine lettuce, torn
1 pt. cherry tomatoes, halved
1 c. mayonnaise-type salad
   dressing
3½ T. sugar
1¼ T. vinegar
¾ lb. bacon, crisply cooked and
   crumbled

Combine broccoli, lettuce and tomatoes in a large bowl. Combine salad dressing, sugar and vinegar in a separate medium bowl; pour over lettuce mixture and toss to coat. Sprinkle with bacon. Chill before serving. Serves 8.

Coli Harrington
Delaware, OH

no-spill salads

Tote creamy salads to potlucks the no-spill way…packed in a large plastic zipping bag. When you arrive, simply pour the salad into a serving bowl.

Fabulous Feta Salad

Make this salad into a main dish by topping with cooked chicken.

5-oz. pkg. spring-blend
    salad mix
½ c. chopped pecans, toasted
¾ c. crumbled feta cheese
6 slices bacon, crisply cooked
    and crumbled

11-oz. can mandarin oranges,
    drained and halved
grated Parmesan cheese to taste
Poppy Seed Dressing

Divide salad mix equally among 4 serving plates; top each with equal servings of pecans, feta cheese, bacon and mandarin oranges. Sprinkle with Parmesan cheese; drizzle with Poppy Seed Dressing. Serve immediately. Serves 4.

Poppy Seed Dressing:

½ c. mayonnaise
⅓ c. sugar
2 T. cider vinegar

¼ c. milk
1 T. poppy seed

Whisk together mayonnaise and sugar; whisk in vinegar and remaining ingredients.

Jen Sell
Farmington, MN

Panzanella Bread Salad

This Italian bread salad includes the traditional ingredients: tomatoes, olive oil, vinegar and seasonings. Fresh ingredients are key to this tasty salad.

4 c. Italian bread, torn into
   bite-size pieces
5 tomatoes, diced
½ red onion, sliced
½ cucumber, peeled, quartered
   and sliced

½ c. fresh basil, chopped
3 cloves garlic, minced
3 T. red wine vinegar
¼ cup olive oil
½ t. salt
½ t. pepper

Combine first 6 ingredients; toss well. Sprinkle with vinegar, oil, salt and pepper. Let stand at room temperature 1½ to 2 hours before serving so the bread can absorb the dressing. Serves 4 to 6.

Annmarie Heavey
Bridgewater, MA

"This traditional Italian bread salad began as a thrifty way to use up day-old bread. Now we make it just because it's delicious!"

Annmarie

Southwest Salad Twist

This colorful cold salad looks and tastes delicious. It's also good as a topping over grilled chicken or fish or as an appetizer with tortilla chips.

1 c. frozen corn, thawed
15-oz. can black beans, drained and rinsed
3 to 4 tomatoes, finely chopped
¼ c. green onions, chopped
¼ c. fresh cilantro, chopped
1 T. chopped green chiles
juice of 1 to 2 limes

Stir together all ingredients except lime juice. Drizzle lime juice over top; gently stir. Serves 4 to 6.

Deborah Thorpe
Tucson, AZ

creative salad bowls

Ripe red tomatoes make delicious salad bowls. Cut a slice from the top of the tomato and use a spoon to scoop out the seeds. Cut the tomato edge into scallops or a zigzag pattern, sprinkle with salt, invert on paper towels and chill. Fill right before serving.

California Cobb Salad

Cobb salad was made famous in Hollywood at the Brown Derby Restaurant. This version is dressed with ranch dressing instead of vinaigrette.

1 head lettuce, shredded
3 c. cooked turkey, cubed
8 slices bacon, crisply cooked
   and crumbled
3 eggs, hard-boiled, peeled and
   sliced

2 tomatoes, chopped
1 avocado, peeled, pitted and
   diced
¾ c. crumbled blue cheese
1 c. green onions, chopped
8-oz. bottle ranch salad dressing

Divide lettuce among 4 to 6 salad plates. Layer turkey and next 6 ingredients over lettuce. Drizzle with dressing to taste. Serves 4 to 6.

Carrie O'Shea
Marina Del Rey, CA

"Always popular at luncheons... simply arrange the ingredients in attractive rows on a single large platter."

Carrie

salad supper

Invite friends over for a Salad Supper on a day that's too hot to cook. Ask everyone to bring along a favorite salad. You provide crispy bread sticks or a basket of tea muffins and a pitcher of iced tea...relax and enjoy!

Southwestern Layered Salad

A rainbow of colors appears in the layers of this bean and vegetable salad, so be sure to serve it in a clear glass bowl for an impressive presentation.

15-oz. can black beans, drained
    and rinsed
¼ c. salsa
2 c. lettuce, chopped
2 tomatoes, chopped
15¼-oz. can corn, drained

1 green pepper, chopped
1 red onion, finely chopped
½ c. shredded Cheddar cheese
¼ c. bacon bits
1 c. ranch salad dressing
Optional: tortilla chips

Combine black beans and salsa in a small bowl. Layer bean mixture, lettuce and next 5 ingredients in a large serving bowl. Sprinkle with bacon bits; drizzle with dressing. Refrigerate until ready to serve. Serve with tortilla chips, if desired. Serves 8.

Lori Downing
Bradenton, FL

"Not only does my family love this recipe, but when I brought it to church I had many requests for it."

Lori

perfect serving bowl

A large glass bowl is a must-have for entertaining. Whether it's used as a salad bowl, pasta dish or filled with water and floating candles, it works beautifully.

Blue Crab Salad

A very flavorful salad that's best served simply...over curly leaf lettuce with your favorite crackers.

6 cloves garlic, minced
2 shallots, minced
¼ c. oil
½ c. sour cream
2-oz. pkg. Boursin cheese,
   softened
1½ t. green hot pepper sauce

¼ t. Worcestershire sauce
1 T. fresh cilantro, chopped
2 T. fresh chives, chopped
juice of 2 limes
1 t. salt
⅛ t. cayenne pepper
1 lb. crabmeat

Sauté garlic and shallots in oil in a skillet over medium-high heat just until translucent; remove from heat. Blend sour cream and Boursin cheese in a mixing bowl; stir in hot pepper sauce, Worcestershire sauce, cilantro and chives. Sprinkle with lime juice, salt and cayenne pepper. Stir in garlic mixture and crabmeat, being careful not to break up the crabmeat too finely. Serves 6 to 8.

Kathy Unruh
Fresno, CA

cool server

An ice bowl makes a cool server for seafood salad. Center a small plastic bowl inside a larger one, using masking tape to hold it in place. Arrange citrus slices and sprigs of mint between the bowls, fill with water and freeze until solid. Gently remove both plastic bowls and fill with salad.

Chinese Chicken Salad

The seasoning packets from the ramen noodles aren't used in this recipe...save them for seasoning soups or casseroles.

4 c. boneless, skinless chicken
    breasts, cooked and diced
1 head cabbage, finely chopped
3 to 4 green onions, chopped
2 to 3 stalks celery, chopped
1 onion, diced

1 red pepper, diced
2 (3-oz.) pkgs. ramen noodles,
    crushed (reserve seasoning
    packets for another use)
Dressing
Garnish: ½ c. sliced almonds

Combine first 7 ingredients in a serving bowl; toss with Dressing. Refrigerate 3 to 4 hours. Sprinkle with almonds before serving, if desired. Serves 8.

Dressing:

¾ c. olive oil
¼ c. sesame oil
6 T. rice vinegar
¼ c. sugar
2 t. salt

2 t. sesame seed
1 t. celery seed
1 t. pepper
Cajun seasoning to taste

Mix together all ingredients in a small bowl.

Joanne Zenker
Annapolis, MD

Orange-Wild Rice Chicken Salad

Heads up! This isn't your ordinary chicken salad…it's better! This salad boasts wild rice, sugar snap peas and mandarin oranges.

6-oz. pkg. long grain and
    wild rice, cooked
2 c. cooked chicken breast,
    shredded
1 c. sugar snap peas, trimmed

15-oz. can mandarin oranges,
    drained
½ c. honey-Dijon salad
    dressing

Combine all ingredients in a large bowl; mix well. Chill until serving time. Serves 4.

Rhonda Reeder
Ellicott City, MD

save the juice

When draining canned fruit, freeze the juice in ice cube trays…oh-so handy for adding a little sweetness to marinades and dressings.

Tuscan Salad

This salad bursts with color and flavor from the freshest ingredients available...including fresh mozzarella cheese. Don't be tempted to substitute regular mozzarella cheese because it's drier and stringier than mild, delicate fresh mozzarella.

1 lb. red and yellow tomatoes, sliced ¼-inch thick	1 t. salt
1 red onion, diced	½ t. freshly ground pepper
4 oranges, peeled and sectioned	Vinaigrette Dressing
1 bunch fresh basil, thinly sliced	16-oz. pkg. fresh mozzarella cheese, diced

Combine first 6 ingredients in a large salad bowl; add Vinaigrette Dressing, tossing gently to coat. Top with mozzarella and serve at room temperature. Serves 6 to 8.

Vinaigrette Dressing:

¼ c. olive oil	¼ t. salt
1 T. balsamic vinegar	¼ t. garlic, minced
1 T. sugar	2 T. water
¼ t. Dijon mustard	

Combine all ingredients in a blender or food processor; process 30 seconds or until smooth.

Helen Eads
Memphis, TN

Extra-Easy Taco Salad

Create a fiesta of your own on nights that you serve this popular Tex-Mex salad. Don't forget favorite accompaniments like sour cream, guacamole and salsa.

1 head lettuce, shredded
2 tomatoes, diced
1 onion, diced
1 green pepper, diced
¾ lb. ground beef, browned

2 c. shredded Cheddar cheese
2 (8-oz.) bottles Catalina salad
   dressing
8-oz. pkg. nacho-flavored tortilla
   chips, coarsely broken

"I sometimes like to add sliced black olives, too...toss in your favorite taco toppers!"

Linda

Mix together all ingredients in a large serving bowl. Serve immediately. Serves 6 to 8.

Linda Day
Wall, NJ

salad croutons

Don't let day-old bread go to waste. Simply cut it into cubes, pack into plastic zipping bags and freeze…it's perfect for making salad croutons or savory stuffing.

Mom's Antipasto Salad

Antipasto *is the Italian word meaning "before the pasta" and is usually served as an appetizer course. But with all the hearty ingredients this salad offers, it can easily stand alone as a main-dish salad.*

1 head lettuce, chopped
½ c. pitted Kalamata olives,
   quartered
½ lb. thick-sliced salami,
   quartered
2 (6-oz.) jars marinated
   artichokes, drained and
   coarsely chopped
1 zucchini, diced
10-oz. pkg. grape tomatoes,
   halved

1 green pepper, chopped
1 red onion, sliced vertically
6 to 8 pepperoncini, coarsely
   chopped
1½ c. grated Parmesan cheese
½ c. Italian salad dressing
5-oz. pkg. garlic-seasoned
   croutons

"Every time I take this to a church potluck my bowl comes back empty! I love to make people happy with my cooking."

Yvonne

   Combine first 10 ingredients; toss gently. Chill until serving time. Just before serving, add dressing to taste; top with croutons. Serves 10.

Yvonne Van Brimmer
Apple Valley, CA

Greek Pasta Salad

Feta cheese, black olives and red peppers lend the Greek flavor to this pasta salad.

16-oz. pkg. rainbow rotini, uncooked
16-oz. pkg. frozen California-blend vegetables, cooked
16-oz. bottle Italian salad dressing
14-oz. can quartered artichoke hearts, drained
12-oz. pkg. sliced pepperoni
10-oz. pkg. crumbled feta cheese
4-oz. can black olives, drained and chopped
½ c. pesto
1 c. cherry tomatoes
1 red pepper, sliced

Cook rotini according to package directions; drain and rinse with cold water.

Combine rotini and vegetables in a large bowl; toss with salad dressing. Add artichoke hearts and remaining ingredients; mix well. Chill overnight; stir before serving. Serves 12.

Lisa Seymour
Blooming Prairie, MN

packing a tossed salad

Put the dressing in the bottom of your container and top with greens and veggies. At mealtime, just stir or shake for a crisp salad every time.

Creamy Garden Coleslaw

Save time by picking up packages of shredded coleslaw mix.

1 head cabbage, shredded
1 zucchini, shredded
1 c. carrots, peeled and grated
½ c. green pepper, chopped
¾ c. mayonnaise

2 T. sugar
1 T. lemon juice
1 t. celery seed
1 t. salt

Combine all ingredients in a large bowl; toss lightly. Cover and chill 15 to 20 minutes. Makes 13 cups.

Jackie Crough
Salina, KS

Peanutty Slaw

The crunch of peanuts complements the bites of crisp cauliflower and cabbage in this slaw. The addition of Parmesan cheese enhances its flavor.

4 c. cabbage, shredded
1 c. cauliflower, chopped
1 c. sour cream
1 c. mayonnaise
1 T. sugar
1 T. vinegar
1 t. salt

½ c. cucumber, chopped
¼ c. green onions, chopped
¼ c. green pepper, chopped
1 T. butter or margarine, melted
½ c. Spanish peanuts
2 T. grated Parmesan cheese

"Great for toting to any get-together... always a must-have!"

Judy

Combine cabbage and cauliflower; set aside. Mix together sour cream and next 7 ingredients; stir into cabbage mixture. Stir together butter, peanuts and cheese; add to cabbage mixture. Serves 8 to 10.

Judy Forgey
Edmonds, WA

Chocolate Chip-Oatmeal
Cookies, page 278

short & sweet
desserts

Enjoy a sweet ending to the meal every night of the week with
this enticing collection of quick & easy desserts. You'll find
make-ahead desserts like Trish's Peanut Butter Pie (page 293).
It chills for only 30 minutes…so it's ready right after supper.

Turn to page 274 to learn how to
make homemade peanut brittle…in
the microwave. It doesn't get
much easier than that! So
satisfy your family's sweet
tooth with any of these
delectable sweets that are
also oh-so simple.

Angel Kisses

Mini chocolate chips and pecans are folded into these delicate meringue cookies. Simply prepare them the night before and bake at a very low temperature for 2 hours; then turn the oven off and let the kisses sit overnight in the oven...don't peek as they cool in the oven.

2 egg whites, at room
   temperature
½ c. sugar
1 t. almond extract

¼ t. vanilla extract
1 c. mini chocolate chips
1 c. chopped pecans

Beat egg whites until foamy; blend in sugar until stiff. Add extracts; blend well. Fold in chocolate chips and pecans. Drop by teaspoonfuls onto parchment paper-lined baking sheets. Bake at 200 degrees for 2 hours; turn oven off. Let meringues stand in closed oven 8 hours or overnight. Makes about 2½ dozen.

JoLisa McCarthy
Bolton, MA

Microwave Peanut Brittle

No candy thermometer is needed for this truly quick & easy candy, but be sure to have all your ingredients and baking sheet ready to go, as you need to work quickly. This peanut brittle was tested in an 1100-watt microwave oven.

1½ c. unsalted dry-roasted
   peanuts
1 c. sugar
½ c. corn syrup

½ t. salt
1 T. butter
1 t. vanilla extract
1 t. baking soda

Mix first 4 ingredients in a large microwave-safe bowl. Microwave on high 6 minutes or until mixture is bubbly and peanuts are lightly browned. Quickly stir in butter and vanilla; microwave 2 minutes. Add baking soda and stir quickly until mixture is foamy. Pour immediately onto a large buttered baking sheet or jelly-roll pan. Cool and break into pieces; store in an airtight container. Makes 14 to 16 servings.

Susie Montag
Richlands, NC

Irresistible Caramel Bars

Send these caramel bars over the top by serving them with a scoop of vanilla ice cream and a drizzle of caramel sauce.

¾ c. butter-flavored shortening
3 c. brown sugar, packed
3 eggs, beaten
1 T. vanilla extract

1¾ c. all-purpose flour
1 T. baking powder
½ t. salt
1 c. chopped nuts

Blend together shortening and brown sugar in a large bowl. Blend in eggs and vanilla; mix well and set aside.

Stir together flour, baking powder and salt; add to shortening mixture, blending until combined. Stir in nuts. Spread in a greased and floured 13"x9" baking pan. Bake at 350 degrees for 35 to 40 minutes. Cool and cut into bars. Makes 1½ to 2 dozen.

Linda Gable
Dublin, OH

shipping cookies

Place pieces of wax paper between cookie layers and add mini marshmallows to make sure cookies don't move around. Tuck in a couple of packages of cocoa for a great gift!

Grace's No-Bake Fudge Squares

A thick layer of chocolatey frosting covers these make-ahead treats.

½ c. brown sugar, packed
1 egg, beaten
½ c. butter
2 c. graham cracker crumbs

½ c. sweetened flaked coconut
½ c. chopped nuts
Buttery Cocoa Frosting

Combine brown sugar, egg and butter in a saucepan over low heat; bring to a boil and cook one minute. Remove from heat and quickly stir in cracker crumbs, coconut and nuts. Immediately press into a greased 8"x8" baking pan. Chill until firm. Spread with Buttery Cocoa Frosting; chill again until firm. Cut into squares. Serves 16.

Buttery Cocoa Frosting:

¼ c. butter
3 T. water
½ t. vanilla extract

3 T. baking cocoa
1 to 2 c. powdered sugar

Melt butter in a saucepan over low heat. Stir in water, vanilla, cocoa and enough powdered sugar to reach desired spreading consistency.

Lisa Hains
Tipp City, OH

"This recipe was shared by Grace, a dear friend of my grandmother. These are quick to make and oh-so yummy! They freeze well for unexpected company...but you may have to hide them!"

Lisa

Chocolate Chip-Oatmeal Cookies
(pictured on page 272)

Oats give these cookies their crunch, and a whole package of chocolate chips gives them their chocolate punch!

¾ c. shortening
1 c. brown sugar, packed
½ c. sugar
1 egg, beaten
¼ c. water
1 t. vanilla extract
1 c. all-purpose flour

1 t. salt
½ t. baking soda
3 c. quick-cooking oats, uncooked
12-oz. pkg. semi-sweet chocolate chips

Blend together first 6 ingredients in a large bowl; add flour, salt and baking soda, blending until combined. Stir in oats and chocolate chips. Drop by teaspoonfuls onto greased baking sheets. Bake at 350 degrees for 10 minutes. Makes about 3½ dozen.

Terri Moore
Asheville, NC

helping hands

Baking cookies is a great activity for first-time cooks. Even the youngest children can help by dropping chocolate chips into the mixing bowl or scooping out spoonfuls of dough. Enjoying the baked cookies will encourage your little helpers to learn more in the kitchen.

Cale's Corn Flake Cookies

Enjoy the crunch of cereal any time of day in these sweet, peanut buttery cookies.

1 c. light corn syrup
1 c. creamy peanut butter
1 c. sugar

1 t. vanilla extract
6 to 7 c. corn flake cereal

Combine all ingredients except cereal in a heavy saucepan; cook over low heat, stirring constantly, until peanut butter is melted and sugar is dissolved. Add cereal and stir well. Drop by teaspoonfuls onto wax paper. Let stand until set. Makes 2 dozen.

Lori Hobscheidt
Washington, IA

Mom & Me Peanut Butter Kisses

With only 4 ingredients, these classic peanut butter & chocolate cookies are easy to make and a good way to get the young ones involved in the baking process. Have them roll the dough into balls and place a chocolate drop in the center.

1 c. creamy peanut butter
1 c. sugar
1 egg

24 milk chocolate drops, unwrapped

Combine peanut butter, sugar and egg in a bowl; mix well. Roll into small balls and arrange on an ungreased baking sheet. Bake at 350 degrees for 12 minutes. Remove from oven; immediately place a chocolate drop in the center of each cookie. Makes about 2 dozen.

Nicole Wrigley
Vancouver, WA

"My mom and I first made these for the holidays...but they were so good, we make them year 'round now!"

Nicole

Sweet Hummingbird Cake

This streamlined version of the popular cake starts with a cake mix, bakes in a Bundt® pan and is finished off with store-bought vanilla frosting...The results? A moist, rich cake that's simple to make.

8-oz. can crushed pineapple
½ c. ripe banana, mashed
¼ c. milk
2 eggs
1 t. vanilla extract

Optional: ¼ c. dark rum
18½-oz. pkg. banana cake mix
16-oz. can vanilla frosting
toasted pecans, chopped

Beat together first 5 ingredients and rum, if desired, in a large mixing bowl at low speed with an electric mixer until blended. Add cake mix; beat at medium speed 2 minutes. Pour batter into a greased and floured Bundt® pan. Bake at 350 degrees for 50 minutes or until a toothpick inserted in center comes out clean. Cool in pan on a wire rack 15 minutes; remove cake from pan and cool completely on wire rack.

Microwave frosting on high 15 to 20 seconds or until pourable. Let stand one minute before drizzling over cake. Sprinkle pecans over frosting. Serves 16.

Wendy Lee Paffenroth
Pine Island, NY

"homemade frosting"

For easy-to-make frosting that's not too sweet, simply blend together a 16-ounce can of frosting with an 8-ounce package of softened cream cheese.

Chocolate Chip-Pudding Cake

That's right...3 chocolate ingredients are all it takes to whip up this extra chocolatey sheet cake.

3½-oz. pkg. cook & serve
    chocolate pudding mix
18.25-oz. pkg. chocolate
    cake mix

12-oz. pkg. semi-sweet
    chocolate chips

Prepare and cook pudding mix according to package directions. Remove pudding from stove top and stir in dry cake mix until just combined. Spread mixture in a greased and floured 13"x9" baking dish. Sprinkle with chocolate chips. Bake at 325 degrees for 30 to 35 minutes. Makes 14 to 16 servings.

Beth Barchesky
Latrobe, PA

Hawaiian Cake

Crushed pineapple and garnishes of coconut and cherries add to the tropical flavor of this simple cake.

18.25-oz. pkg. white or yellow
    cake mix
8-oz. pkg. cream cheese,
    softened
2 c. milk
3.4-oz. pkg. instant vanilla
    pudding mix

20-oz. can crushed pineapple,
    drained
16-oz. container frozen whipped
    topping, thawed
Garnishes: toasted coconut,
    chopped nuts, sliced
    maraschino cherries

Prepare cake mix according to package directions. Pour into a greased 13"x9" baking pan and bake at 350 degree for 15 minutes; cool. Combine cream cheese, milk and pudding mix; blend until fluffy.

Stir in pineapple. Spread mixture evenly over top of cake; cover with whipped topping. Sprinkle with coconut, nuts and cherries, if desired. Chill until ready to serve. Serves 8 to 10.

Jackie Crough
Salina, KS

Grandma K's Coffee Cake

You'll discover a sugary layer of cinnamon and nuts inside the cake...and sprinkled on top!

½ c. butter or margarine, softened	2 eggs, beaten
1 c. sugar	1 c. sour cream
1 t. vanilla extract	1½ c. all-purpose flour
¼ t. salt	1 t. baking soda
	Topping, divided

Blend together first 4 ingredients in a mixing bowl. Add eggs and mix well. Add sour cream, flour and baking soda. Pour half of batter into a greased 13"x9" baking pan; sprinkle with half of Topping. Pour other half of batter into pan and top with the remaining Topping. Bake at 325 degrees for 30 minutes. Makes 16 to 18 servings.

Topping:

½ c. sugar	1½ t. cinnamon
¼ c. chopped nuts	

Mix together all ingredients in a small bowl.

Sharon Timmerman
Aviston, IL

"My grandma always made this coffee cake for a treat when my mom & my aunt came to help her put a new quilt in the frame...it became known as Grandma K's Quilting Coffee Cake."

Sharon

Peanut Butter Texas Sheet Cake

Attention, peanut butter lovers! This moist cake has peanut butter baked inside the cake and mixed into the icing…plus a sprinkling of peanuts on top!

2 c. all-purpose flour
2 c. sugar
½ t. salt
1 t. baking soda
1 c. butter
1 c. water

¼ c. creamy peanut butter
2 eggs, beaten
1 t. vanilla extract
½ c. buttermilk
Peanut Butter Icing
Garnish: chopped peanuts

Combine flour, sugar, salt and baking soda in a large bowl; set aside. Combine butter, water and peanut butter in a saucepan over medium heat; bring to a boil. Add to flour mixture and mix well; set aside. Combine eggs, vanilla and buttermilk; add to peanut butter mixture.

Spread batter in a greased 15"x10" jelly-roll pan. Bake at 350 degrees for 25 to 28 minutes or until cake springs back when gently touched. Spread Peanut Butter Icing over warm cake and garnish, if desired. Serves 15 to 20.

Peanut Butter Icing:

½ c. butter
¼ c. creamy peanut butter
⅓ c. plus 1 T. milk

16-oz. pkg. powdered sugar
1 t. vanilla extract

Combine first 3 ingredients in a saucepan over medium heat; bring to a boil. Remove from heat; stir in powdered sugar and vanilla, mixing until spreading consistency.

Kathi Rostash
Nevada, OH

Turtle Cake

German chocolate cake mix, caramels and nuts are the hallmarks of this gooey cake. This version adds even more flavor with a cup of chocolate chips.

18½-oz. pkg. German chocolate cake mix
14-oz. pkg. caramels, unwrapped
½ c. evaporated milk
½ c. butter or margarine
1 c. chopped walnuts
1 c. semi-sweet chocolate chips

Prepare cake mix according to package directions; pour half of the batter into a greased and floured 13"x9" baking pan. Bake at 350 degrees for 15 minutes.

Melt caramels, milk and butter in a saucepan; blend well and spread over baked cake. Sprinkle with walnuts and chocolate chips; pour remaining batter over top. Bake for 20 more minutes; cool. Serves 8 to 12.

Laura Strausberger
Cary, IL

edible centerpiece

A heaping plate of cookies, bars, cupcakes or cake squares makes a delightful (and delicious) centerpiece at a casual gathering with friends.

Ooey-Gooey Butter Cake

Powdered sugar and cream cheese jazz up a store-bought cake mix...
resulting in ooey-gooey delight!

18½-oz. pkg. yellow cake mix
4 eggs, divided
½ c. butter, softened

16-oz. pkg. powdered sugar
8-oz. pkg. cream cheese,
  softened

"Yum says it all!"

Gayla

   Mix together cake mix, 2 eggs and butter; spread in a greased 13"x9" baking pan. Combine powdered sugar, cream cheese and remaining eggs in a mixing bowl; blend well. Spread over cake mixture; bake at 375 degrees for 40 to 45 minutes. Cool; cut into squares. Makes 24.

Gayla Weltzer
Camden, OH

extra special

For a little something extra on cakes and brownies, try topping with chopped candy bars. Make chopping a breeze when you wrap them in plastic and freeze for 10 to 15 minutes beforehand.

Crustless Coconut Pie

The beauty of this recipe is that it makes 2 pies…one to keep and one to give away.

4 eggs
1¾ c. sugar
2 c. milk
¼ c. butter, melted

½ c. self-rising flour
1 t. vanilla extract
1 c. flaked coconut, divided

"The ultimate dessert when you discover you don't have a pie crust on hand!"
Glenda

Beat eggs at medium speed with an electric mixer until frothy. Add sugar and next 4 ingredients; beat well. Place ½ cup coconut in each of 2 shallow, lightly greased 9" pie plates; pour half of filling mixture into each pie plate, stirring gently to distribute coconut. Bake at 350 degrees for 25 to 30 minutes or until golden. Makes 2 pies.

Glenda Geohagen
DeFuniak Springs, FL

make it special

Set out whipped cream and shakers of cinnamon and cocoa at dessert time for coffee drinkers. Tea drinkers will love a basket of special teas with honey and lemon slices. Special desserts deserve the best!

Lemonade Pie

Make any flavor you like by substituting a different flavor of frozen fruit drink concentrate...try orange or raspberry.

1 qt. vanilla ice cream, softened   9-inch graham cracker crust
6-oz. can frozen lemonade
   concentrate, softened

Combine ice cream and lemonade concentrate. Spoon into crust and freeze at least 4 hours or until firm. Let stand at room temperature a few minutes before serving. Serves 6 to 8.

Staci Meyers
Cocoa, FL

sweet offering

For an oh-so-pretty gift, top pies with an inverted pie plate and secure both together with a bandanna.

Tennessee Fudge Pie

No fudge pie would be complete without a scoop of ice cream!

2 eggs, beaten
½ c. butter, melted and cooled
¼ c. baking cocoa
¼ c. all-purpose flour
1 c. sugar

2 t. vanilla extract
⅓ c. semi-sweet chocolate chips
⅓ c. chopped pecans
9-inch pie crust

Beat together eggs and butter in a large bowl. Add cocoa and remaining ingredients except pie crust; mix well. Pour into pie crust. Bake at 350 degrees for 25 minutes or until firm. Serves 8.

Dusty Jones
Paxton, IL

"My mama has always made this pie for Thanksgiving and people request it for church socials, parties and family suppers. It's a chocolate lover's dream!"

Dusty

homemade goodness

Add a dollop of homemade whipped cream to pie and cake slices...it's a snap to make and tastes so much better than store-bought. Combine one cup heavy cream with ¼ cup powdered sugar and one teaspoon vanilla extract in a chilled bowl; beat until soft peaks form.

Trish's Peanut Butter Pie

To many, chocolate & peanut butter make for the ultimate pairing of flavors. So if you can't resist, add a drizzle of chocolate sauce to slices of this decadent pie.

½ c. creamy peanut butter
4 oz. cream cheese, softened
½ c. milk
8-oz. container frozen whipped
   topping, thawed

9-inch graham cracker crust
Garnishes: additional whipped
   topping, baking cocoa,
   chopped peanuts

Beat peanut butter and cream cheese in a bowl until creamy. Gradually add milk, beating until smooth. Fold in whipped topping; pour into pie crust. Freeze about 30 minutes. Garnish each serving with a dollop of whipped topping and a sprinkle of cocoa and chopped peanuts, if desired. Store in the refrigerator. Serves 6 to 8.

Trish Gothard
Greenville, KY

pies galore

Consider having a Pie Night. Invite family & friends to bring their favorite pie to share. And don't forget copies of the recipes…someone's sure to ask!

Old Dominion Chess Pie

Think of this as a chocolate pecan pie…yum!

5 T. baking cocoa
1½ c. sugar
2 eggs, beaten
½ c. chopped pecans

¼ c. butter, melted
½ c. evaporated milk
½ c. flaked coconut
9-inch pie crust, unbaked

Mix together first 7 ingredients; pour into pie crust. Bake at 400 degrees for 30 minutes. Cool completely. Serves 6 to 8.

Carol Hickman
Kingsport, TN

appetizing recollections

Stir up sweet memories…look through Grandma's recipe box and rediscover a long-forgotten favorite dessert recipe to share.

Strawberry Pizza

With a sugar cookie crust, a cream cheese "sauce" and fresh strawberry toppings, what's not to like about this dessert pizza? Be creative and add your favorite fruit toppings like kiwi or banana slices or even chocolate curls.

18-oz. tube refrigerated sugar
  cookie dough
8-oz. pkg. cream cheese,
  softened
2 c. frozen whipped topping,
  thawed

1 t. vanilla extract
1 c. powdered sugar
12.75-oz. pkg. strawberry glaze
16-oz. pkg. strawberries, hulled
  and sliced

Roll out dough on a greased 12" pizza pan; bake according to package directions. Let cool.

Mix together cream cheese, whipped topping, vanilla and powdered sugar; spread over cooled crust. Top with glaze and strawberries. Serves 6 to 8.

Micki Stephens
Marion, OH

quick, easy...clean!

To easily clean strawberries, place them in a sink of water and gently wash with the sprayer nozzle on the sink. The water from the nozzle will toss and turn the strawberries, giving them a thorough cleaning.

Quick Blueberry Crisp

Substitute your favorite fruit pie filling to create your own quick version of this fruit crisp.

21-oz. can blueberry pie filling
½ c. rolled oats, uncooked
½ c. all-purpose flour

¼ c. brown sugar, packed
2 T. chopped walnuts
6 T. butter or margarine

Spoon blueberry pie filling into a lightly greased one-quart baking dish. Combine oats, flour, brown sugar and walnuts in a medium mixing bowl. Cut in butter with a pastry blender or 2 knives until mixture resembles coarse crumbs. Sprinkle over pie filling. Bake, uncovered, at 375 degrees for 45 minutes or until lightly browned and bubbly. Makes 4 to 6 servings.

Flo Burtnett
Gage, OK

Peach Melba

To speed the ripening process of peaches, place them in a loosely closed paper bag at room temperature for one to 3 days. Be sure to check them daily because ripening can occur very quickly.

2 peaches, peeled, pitted and
    halved
1 T. lemon juice
1 c. raspberries

1 T. extra-fine sugar
½ t. vanilla extract
½ c. vanilla ice cream, divided

Sprinkle peaches with lemon juice; set aside.

Mash raspberries in a bowl; stir in sugar and vanilla. Arrange 2 peach halves in each serving dish. Top each serving with ¼ cup ice cream; spoon raspberry sauce over ice cream. Serves 2.

*Leslie Stimel
Columbus, OH*

peach of an idea!

Delectable fruit like peaches needn't go to waste if it ripens quicker than you can eat it. Puree, freeze and use later for topping cheesecakes or waffles…or any favorite food.

Mini Maple-Pear Cobblers

Serve these mini cobblers warm with whipped cream and drizzled with additional maple syrup...so good.

3 lbs. pears, cored, peeled and
   quartered
⅔ c. maple syrup
2 T. all-purpose flour
1 t. vanilla extract
¼ t. ground nutmeg
2 T. butter
Topping
Garnishes: melted butter, sugar,
   additional ground nutmeg

Combine first 5 ingredients in a bowl; mix well. Divide mixture among 6 lightly greased custard cups; top each with a pat of butter. Bake at 425 degrees for 18 to 20 minutes.

Drop Topping by spoonfuls onto hot pear mixture. If desired, brush with melted butter and sprinkle with sugar and nutmeg. Bake at 425 degrees for 14 more minutes or until golden. Serves 6.

Topping:

1½ c. all-purpose flour
2¼ t. baking powder
¼ t. ground nutmeg
6 T. butter
9 T. whipped cream
9 T. maple syrup
1 t. vanilla extract

Combine first 3 ingredients in a food processor. Add butter and process until fine crumbs form. Add cream, syrup and vanilla; process until combined.

Karen Pilcher
Burleson, TX

Pears Extraordinaire

These pears are extraordinary because of their flavored cream cheese filling topped with gooey caramel sauce, whipped topping and pecans...a truly spectacular treat.

2 pears, cored and halved
¼ c. apple juice
2 T. cream cheese, softened
2 T. honey
2 t. brown sugar, packed

½ t. vanilla extract
4 t. caramel ice cream topping
4 T. frozen whipped topping, thawed
4 t. chopped pecans

Arrange pear halves, cut-side down, in a microwave-safe dish. Drizzle with apple juice. Cover and microwave on high 5 minutes or until pears are tender; set aside.

Mix together cream cheese, honey, brown sugar and vanilla until creamy and smooth. Arrange pears, cut-side up, on 4 serving plates. Spoon one-quarter of cream cheese mixture in the center of each pear. Drizzle each serving with one teaspoon caramel ice cream topping, dollop with whipped topping and sprinkle one teaspoon pecans over top. Serves 4.

Susan Metzger
Washougal, WA

Creamy Banana Pudding

Whipped topping and chunks of vanilla wafers top this creamy pudding. It's a crowd-pleaser in both flavor and quantity.

12 oz. cream cheese, softened
1½ (5.1-oz.) pkgs. instant vanilla
   pudding mix
4½ c. milk, divided
1½ t. vanilla extract
12-oz. container frozen whipped
   topping, thawed

12-oz. pkg. vanilla wafers,
   coarsely crushed
4 bananas, sliced
Optional: additional whipped
   topping, vanilla wafers
   broken into large pieces

Process cream cheese, pudding mix, 2½ cups milk and vanilla in a food processor or blender until smooth. Pour into a large bowl; whisk in remaining milk.

Whisk whipped topping into pudding mixture. Layer crushed vanilla wafers, banana slices and pudding mixture in a 4-quart casserole dish. Top with additional whipped topping and vanilla wafers, if desired. Chill at least 4 hours before serving. Serves 10 to 12.

Elizabeth Cox
Lewisville, TX

toasted coconut

Make a good thing even better…sprinkle toasted coconut over banana pudding. Spread about ½ cup shredded coconut in a shallow pan and bake at 350 degrees for 5 minutes or until golden, stirring frequently.

Microwave Chocolate Pudding

This make-ahead dessert is the perfect ending to casual meals year 'round.

⅔ c. sugar
¼ c. baking cocoa
3 T. cornstarch
¼ t. salt

2¼ c. milk
2 T. butter, softened
1 t. vanilla extract

Combine first 4 ingredients in a microwave-safe mixing bowl; gradually stir in milk. Microwave on high 6 minutes, stirring every 2 minutes. Stir in butter and vanilla until smooth.

Divide pudding into 4 individual serving dishes; press plastic wrap directly onto surface of pudding in each dish. Chill 3 to 4 hours. Serves 4.

Justina Montoya
Belen, NM

No-Fry Fried Ice Cream

This quick & easy dessert features ice cream balls rolled in a crunchy cereal topping…mimicking the familiar Mexican ice cream dessert.

6 c. honey-coated corn flake
   cereal, crushed
2 T. sugar
3 T. butter or margarine, melted
5 T. corn syrup
1 t. cinnamon

1 gal. vanilla ice cream,
   softened
Garnishes: caramel ice cream
   topping, whipped topping,
   additional cinnamon

Combine first 5 ingredients; set aside.

Shape ice cream into 3-inch balls; roll in cereal mixture, pressing mixture lightly to coat balls. Place ice cream balls in muffin tins; freeze until ready to serve. To serve, place each ice cream ball in a serving dish, drizzle with caramel topping, dollop with whipped topping and sprinkle with additional cinnamon, if desired. Makes 8.

Renee Lewis
Basin, WY

we all scream for ice cream!

Celebrate National Ice Cream Month…it's the whole month of July! A fun-filled reason to enjoy all your frosty favorites with friends & family.

meals in minutes

company's coming

serves 6

*Zesty Roasted
Chicken & Potatoes
(page 123)*

**Green Beans with Bacon & Garlic
(page 235)*

salad supper

serves 6 to 8

*Blue Crab Salad
(page 262)*

*Crispy Parmesan Pita Crackers
(page 22)*

*Double recipe.

breakfast for dinner

serves 8

Ranch House Burritos
(page 87)

*Golden Home Fries
(page 98)

spring fling

serves 4

Pepper-Crusted Salmon
(page 155)

Savory Orzo Dish
(page 242)

Garlic Roasted Asparagus
(page 234)

summer supper

serves 8

Janet Sue's Crab Cakes
(page 158)

*Lemon-Rice Pilaf
(page 246)

steamed broccoli

tex-mex night

serves 4

Vickie's Gazpacho Dip
(page 10)

Fiesta Beef Fajitas
(page 187)

No-Fry Fried Ice Cream
(page 305)

*Double recipe.

down-home comfort

serves 6 to 8

Saucy Meatloaf
(page 143)

Loaded Baked Potato Casserole
(page 243)

English peas

weeknight favorite

serves 8

Just Perfect Sloppy Joes
(page 189)

Creamy Garden Coleslaw
(page 271)

slow & easy
holiday dinner

serves 6

Holiday Cranberry Pork Roast
(page 180)

Country Cornbread Dressing
(page 169)

roasted Brussels sprouts

lunch with the girls

serves 8

*Chicken Salad Croissants
(page 223)

Marinated Tomatoes
(page 247)

green grapes

*Double recipe.

south-of-the-border breakfast

serves 4

Tex-Mex Scramble
(page 87)

Sausage & Egg Muffins
(page 98)

Italian night

serves 6

Easy Cheesy Lasagna
(page 138)

Tuscan Salad
(page 266)

garlic bread

Sunday dinner

serves 4

Lemony "Baked" Chicken
(page 176)

Fabulous Feta Salad
(page 255)

wild rice

grill it up

serves 9

**Ham & Pineapple Kabobs
(page 68)

Citrus-Apple Sweet Potatoes
(page 63)

**Triple recipe.

coastal delight

serves 6 to 8

South Carolina Gumbo
(page 206)

French bread

sandwich night

serves 8

Easy Stromboli
(page 139)

chips

Strawberry Pizza
(page 295)

pantry perfect

Keep these ready-made essentials in your pantry, fridge or freezer to whip up speedy meals from any of our 16 menus on pages 306-313.

fruits & veggies

asparagus
avocados
bell pepper, green
broccoli
Brussels sprouts
cabbage
carrots
celery
cranberries, dried
English peas
green beans
green chiles (canned)
green grapes
lemon juice
lemons
lettuce
lime juice
mandarin oranges, canned
mushrooms, sliced
okra
onions: green, red & white
orange juice
oranges
pineapple chunks (canned)
potatoes: baking & redskin
raisins
shallots
spring-blend salad mix

strawberries
sweet potatoes
tomatoes with chiles (canned)
tomatoes: red and yellow
zucchini

sauces & soups

cream of chicken soup
green hot pepper sauce
jellied cranberry sauce
picante sauce
red steak sauce
savory herb soup mix
soy sauce

spaghetti sauce
tomato sauce
Worcestershire sauce

meats

bacon slices
beef skirt
chicken: boneless, skinless
  breasts, cooked & roasting
crabmeat, fresh
ground beef
ham, smoked
pepperoni, sliced
pork: boneless loin roast,
  ground sausage
salmon fillets

rice & pasta

instant rice
long-grain rice
wild rice
orzo
vermicelli
wide egg noodles

breads

cornbread
corn tortillas
croissants
day-old bread
dry bread crumbs
flour tortillas
French bread
frozen bread dough
garlic bread
pita rounds
sandwich buns
soft bread crumbs

dairy

butter or margarine
cheese: Boursin, crumbled feta,
    fresh mozzarella, grated
    Parmesan, shredded sharp
    Cheddar & shredded
    mozzarella
cottage cheese
cream cheese
eggs
milk
sour cream

desserts

caramel ice cream topping
frozen whipped topping
strawberry glaze
refrigerated sugar cookie
    dough
vanilla ice cream

flavor boosters

balsamic vinegar
basil, fresh
black pepper: ground,
    peppercorns
Cajun seasoning
catsup
cayenne pepper
celery seed
chicken broth
chili powder
chives, fresh
cider vinegar
cilantro, fresh
cinnamon
cloves, ground
fajita seasoning mix
garlic: cloves, minced,
    powder & salt
ginger, ground
mayonnaise
mustard: Dijon,
    dry & prepared
oil: canola, olive & vegetable

oregano, dried
paprika
parsley, dried
parsley, fresh
pimentos
sage, dried
salt
seasoned salt
thyme, fresh

miscellaneous

almonds, sliced
applesauce
cornstarch
corn syrup
cranberry juice cocktail
guacamole
honey-coated corn flake cereal
non-stick vegetable spray
potato chips
salsa
sugar: brown, granulated &
    powdered,
vanilla extract

METRIC EQUIVALENTS

The recipes that appear in this cookbook use the standard U.S. method for measuring liquid and dry or solid ingredients (teaspoons, tablespoons, and cups). The information in the following charts is provided to help cooks outside the United States successfully use these recipes. All equivalents are approximate.

METRIC EQUIVALENTS FOR DIFFERENT TYPES OF INGREDIENTS

A standard cup measure of a dry or solid ingredient will vary in weight depending on the type of ingredient.
A standard cup of liquid is the same volume for any type of liquid. Use the following chart when converting standard cup measures to grams (weight) or milliliters (volume).

Standard Cup	Fine Powder (ex. flour)	Grain (ex. rice)	Granular (ex. sugar)	Liquid Solids (ex. butter)	Liquid (ex. milk)
1	140 g	150 g	190 g	200 g	240 ml
¾	105 g	113 g	143 g	150 g	180 ml
⅔	93 g	100 g	125 g	133 g	160 ml
½	70 g	75 g	95 g	100 g	120 ml
⅓	47 g	50 g	63 g	67 g	80 ml
¼	35 g	38 g	48 g	50 g	60 ml
⅛	18 g	19 g	24 g	25 g	30 ml

USEFUL EQUIVALENTS FOR LIQUID INGREDIENTS BY VOLUME

¼ tsp	=			1 ml
½ tsp	=			2 ml
1 tsp	=			5 ml
3 tsp = 1 tbls		= ½ fl oz	=	15 ml
2 tbls	= ⅛ cup	= 1 fl oz	=	30 ml
4 tbls	= ¼ cup	= 2 fl oz	=	60 ml
5⅓ tbls	= ⅓ cup	= 3 fl oz	=	80 ml
8 tbls	= ½ cup	= 4 fl oz	=	120 ml
10⅔ tbls	= ⅔ cup	= 5 fl oz	=	160 ml
12 tbls	= ¾ cup	= 6 fl oz	=	180 ml
16 tbls	= 1 cup	= 8 fl oz	=	240 ml
1 pt	= 2 cups	= 16 fl oz	=	480 ml
1 qt	= 4 cups	= 32 fl oz	=	960 ml
		33 fl oz	=	1000 ml = 1 liter

USEFUL EQUIVALENTS FOR DRY INGREDIENTS BY WEIGHT

(To convert ounces to grams, multiply the number of ounces by 30.)

1 oz	=	¹⁄₁₆ lb	=	30 g
4 oz	=	¼ lb	=	120 g
8 oz	=	½ lb	=	240 g
12 oz	=	¾ lb	=	360 g
16 oz	=	1 lb	=	480 g

USEFUL EQUIVALENTS FOR LENGTH

(To convert inches to centimeters, multiply the number of inches by 2.5.)

1 in =		=	2.5 cm
6 in = ½ ft		=	15 cm
12 in = 1 ft		=	30 cm
36 in = 3 ft	= 1 yd =	90 cm
40 in =		= 100 cm	= 1 meter

USEFUL EQUIVALENTS FOR COOKING/OVEN TEMPERATURES

	Fahrenheit	Celsius	Gas Mark
Freeze Water	32° F	0° C	
Room Temperature	68° F	20° C	
Boil Water	212° F	100° C	
Bake	325° F	160° C	3
	350° F	180° C	4
	375° F	190° C	5
	400° F	200° C	6
	425° F	220° C	7
	450° F	230° C	8
Broil			Grill

index

How did Gooseberry Patch get started?

Back in 1984, we were next-door neighbors raising our families in the little town of Delaware, Ohio. We were two moms with small children looking for a way to do what we loved and stay home with the kids too. We shared a love of home-cooking, vintage kitchenware & antiques and making memories with family & friends. After many a conversation over the backyard fence, Gooseberry Patch was born.

We put together the first catalog & cookbooks at our kitchen tables and packed boxes from the basement, enlisting the help of our loved ones wherever we could. From that little family, we've grown to include an amazing group of creative folks who love cooking, decorating and creating as much as we do. We love hand-picking the selection for our catalog each season and are tickled to share our inspiration, recipes, ideas, photos and more with you.

Some days, we still can't believe it's been over 25 years since those kitchen-table days...we couldn't have done it without our friends all across the country. Whether you've been along for the ride from the beginning or are just discovering us, we're glad you're here!

Your friends at Gooseberry Patch